SATTVIK
Foods of India

ANUPAMA SHUKLA

Illustrations
SUHITA MITRA

Body & Soul Books

ISBN 978-93-81115-94-7
© Anupama Shukla, 2015

Cover, Illustrations & Artworks Suhita Mitra
Printing Repro Knowledgecast Limited, Thane

Published in India, 2015
BODY & SOUL BOOKS
An imprint of
LEADSTART PUBLISHING PVT LTD
Unit 25/26, Building A/1 Near Wadala RTO
Wadala (East), Mumbai 400037, INDIA
T + 91 22 24046887 **F** +91 22 40700800
E info@leadstartcorp.com **W** www.leadstartcorp.com

To Baba ~
the consummate student and teacher

ABOUT THE AUTHOR

Anupama Shukla is a bureaucrat by profession. She grew up in a family that observed many guidelines related to a Sattvik lifestyle, but like most teenagers paid scant attention to them. Growing older, she moved from taking her body (and mind) for granted, to becoming increasingly aware of how what we eat shapes who we are. Her other interests include healing through aromatherapy and Bach Flower Remedies. Anupama can be reached at: anupamadshukla@gmail.com

ABOUT THE ILLUSTRATOR

Suhita Mitra was born in Kohima, Nagaland – a region of untouched, natural beauty. Wherever the eye travelled, there were hills, trees, flowers and wildlife. Television was still unknown and all that young children had to amuse them was the enchantment offered by the gardens, the playing fields and books…lots of story books. Such an environment was a natural nursery for the imagination. Suhita joined the National Institute Of Design, Ahmedabad, where the untrammeled imagination fostered by her childhood environment, suddenly found meaningful channels through art appreciation, photography, freehand drawing, animation and typography. With her love of nature, she feels inspired to give back through her work as an illustrator and designer. Suhita can be reached at: suhita.mitra@gmail.com

CONTENTS

6

7

INTRODUCTION

Overhauling our cooking and eating patterns is not an easy task. After all, our palate has long ruled us and like anyone used to power, is reluctant to relinquish control. Keeping this in view, the recipes presented here are relatively easy to prepare, tasty and nourishing. As you make these dishes, you will find the particular combinations and proportions of seasonings, spices and herbs that suit you individually. The important fact to remember is that anything in excess is harmful and even *sattvik* food consumed unwisely will have a *tamasik* effect. Moderation is therefore crucial.

When the craving for less preferable food options strikes (such as fried foods) – and it will – opt for homemade snacks, made with love, offered to the Divine and consumed fresh. More importantly, live in the present and do not wallow in guilt about having eaten something that was not in accordance with these principles. Instead of thinking of what you should not have eaten, engage actively in preparing food that you know is good for you. With time, the desire for food that does not suit you will certainly wane, provided you make simple, fresh and balanced dishes the basic framework for your daily diet. Our bodies are always speaking to us – its just that we do not often stop to listen. So it is time to let a rewarding dialogue begin.

As far as possible, avoid leftovers since these are *tamasik*. Ideally, food should be consumed within 4 hours of cooking. This is difficult for most of us in the beginning, so aim to prepare food that is consumed the same day. However, in most cases, food made at home (even leftovers), will be far less harmful than anything made and sold commercially. Finally, always eat in meditative silence and never hurry a meal.

YOU ARE WHAT YOU EAT

From food, verily, are produced all creatures – whatsoever dwell on earth. By food alone, furthermore, do they live and to food, in the end, do they return; for food alone is the eldest of all beings and therefore, it is called the panacea for all. ~ Taittiriya Upanishad

Food is an integral constituent of our daily lives, without which, physical existence as we know it, would be impossible. Without food, we could not *be*, and yet, we tend to approach food in a mechanical and routine manner. It was not always so. Across ancient cultures, there was a deep sense of reverence for all forms of sustenance. Processes related to the procurement of food – for instance the sowing, reaping and threshing of grain or the rearing of livestock, was clearly defined. Somewhere along the way, to our disadvantage, we lost the connection to the food we consume and the processes that bring it to our kitchens and dining tables.

10   One of the single most basic requirements of our existence, thinking about food, occupies much of our waking time but not in the sense of consciously aware thinking. Depending on the mood, mealtimes are approached either mechanically, almost without thought, or with great anticipation, focusing mainly on the gratification of the palate. Either way, we meander through the exercise of the preparation and consumption of food – an attitude that has led to severely detrimental effects not just on the natural world around us, but also on our bodies and minds. In fact, till we rectify the imbalances within ourselves at the physical and mental levels, our attempts at setting right the chaos we have caused on this planet, will be of limited value.

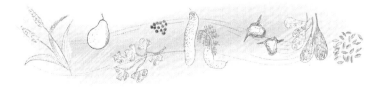

The Ayurvedic Perspective on Food

Ancient India keenly observed human life and the surrounding cosmos, and concluded that 'we are what we eat'. To understand the different ways that food affects our mind, body and soul, it is essential to touch briefly upon the fundamentals enunciated by Ayurveda – the science of life contained in the *Atharva Veda*. According to Ayurveda, all material and non-material matter is constituted of the *Panchamahabhuta*s or five elements: Akash, Vayu, Tejas, Prithvi and Ap. They are the building blocks for everything and provide the link between us and the world we are surrounded by. Through food, we are the water, air, sunshine, and all that exists. We are the universe and the universe is us. This appreciation of the commonality that all existence shares, allowed older cultures to see that our being is, at every level, intricately fashioned by the food we eat. In other words, if we want to change anything about ourselves, and this is not limited to the purely physical, we need to alter our diet.

However, modification of food habits is something most of us are loth to do. We are creatures of comfort, generally unwilling to change anything familiar and food provides both succour and pleasure. To us, food is or rather appears to be, an effective tool that distracts us from pain and sorrow, and enhances what we identify as states of happiness and satisfaction. While the actual definitions of these states of mind and heart may well have differing individual interpretations, it is worthwhile to dwell on the tremendous impact that the food we consume has on every minute of our lives. Many of us have grown used to indifferent states of health. We accept that our busy lives do not leave enough time to 'look after ourselves' in the way that we would like to and so feeling below par in some way or other i.e. physically, mentally or emotionally, every now and then.

Other than on the physical level, most of us never relate the way we feel to the food we eat. If at all this occurs to us, our observations are limited to the immediate effects of food such as when something tasty but spicy causes acidity or a rich dessert leaves us feeling lethargic and sluggish. These occasions generally find us reaching for some OTC remedy to ameliorate the offending symptoms but rarely do we pause to register the subtle signals sent out by the body and ponder the messages transmitted by it after we have eaten. In all

11

probability, this is because we know that to question whether we are eating right would mean acknowledging the need for change and change in this direction is particularly difficult. Worthwhile yes, easy no.

The five basic elements or *Panchamahabhutas*, are fundamental to understanding the relationship between the cosmos and its constituents. Briefly, each element is connected to different organs and reflects its attributes on the human body. *Akash* or ether, for instance, is the space that allows all other elements to exist. Within our bodies, it is the organs that have space within, such as the lungs, stomach and bladder that are predominantly associated with this element. *Vayu* or air, is the element that provides movement. It can be called 'ether in motion'. It is the basis of everything that moves within our systems, including the thoughts that flit across our minds and the movement of food in our digestive tracts. *Tejas* is universal fire. It provides light and illumination within the mind. Within our bodies it converts the food we consume into the energy that we need to live. Too much of this element will cause more heat than necessary and too little will mean that food we eat changes character far too slowly for it to be of any use to us. *Ap* is water, the primary constituent of our bodies, as also of the planet we live on. It is the universal cleanser and detoxifier. *Prithvi* or earth, is what provides solidity to the world and our bodies. On our planet it is the soil and rocks, heavy and unyielding. In our bodies it manifests as bones, teeth and the skeletal framework.

The food we eat, also being made up of these elements, it stands to reason that our bodies will be affected by what we eat. Nourishment predominant in one element will be fine as long as our natural constitution is lacking in that element, but should that not be the case, prolonged consumption of the wrong food will be the starting point for imbalances and later chronic disease.

Tridosha

The *Panchamahabhuta*s combine to form the three *Doshas* – *Vata*, *Pitta* and *Kapha*. The Sanskrit word *dosha*, is commonly understood as 'fault'. The term is indicative of the fact that these are qualities that can easily become 'out of balance' i.e. at fault. According to Ayurveda, while all three forces are present in each person, one or two of the three *doshas* tend to be predominant in each individual. People having constitutions with a balance of all three *doshas* also exist, but for most of us, the constitutions are dominated by one or a mix of any two of the three *doshas*. Hence, the descriptions of constitutions or personalities from the Ayurvedic perspective are given as: i. *Vitta*-type (V), ii. *Pitta*-type (P), iii. *Kapha*-type (K) OR iv.*Vata-Pitta* (V-P) type, v. *Pitta-Kapha* (P-K), vi. Vata-Kapha(V-K) OR viii. the Vata-Pitta-Kapha (V-P-K) personality. The physical make-up and other attributes of the individual also reflect the qualities of the dominant *dosha*/s. It is well worth visiting an Ayurvedic physician to help determine the dominant dosha/s for your personality or constitution.

Vata is a combination of Air and Ether and represents the kinetic energies of the system. It is primarily associated with all movement in and of the mind and body. It affects the nervous system. The chief characteristic associated with it is dryness, which appears in the body or mind only when *Vata* has increased.
Pitta is a combination of Fire and Water and represents the balance between the kinetic and potential energies. It is the force behind all transformation and assimilation and thus has more to do with digestion, whether of food or thought. The chief characteristic associated with it is heat. When heat increases, the body show inflammation and irritability of mind.
Kapha is a combination of Water and Earth and represents potential energy. It relates to the stability and lubrication of the body. The chief characteristic associated with it is heaviness. Increase of *Kapha* reflects as slowness and lethargy of mind and body.

13

Prana: the Key to Better Health
To better understand the factors that influence the beginning or continuation of the imbalances that commonly plague our systems, we need to look at *Prana*. From the Vedic perspective; energy, light and matter are the three primary manifestations of the ultimate consciousness and *Prana* is the breath or life-force or energy, which sustains consciousness in the material world. Food is the primary channel through which *prana* enters the body. It follows therefore, that the more *Prana* our food contains, the higher will be the energy we possess, the better the overall quality of life and the greater the synchronicity with the world around us. Given the range of *Prana*'s operations, from the gross to the subtle,

this also means that the level of consciousness we operate from depends on what we eat. Thus, lack of thought towards the food we eat, inevitably leads to a disconnect with our consciousness. We can still go through life, but in a mechanical way, battling through days that seem weighed down by lethargy, aches and pains.

To increase the level of *Prana* in our lives, we need to start eating right i.e. consume food that has a sufficient amount of *prana*. Let us look at how *Prana* enters food and how it is reduced in food. *Prana* enters our bodies and all life forms through the *Panchamahabhutas*. In the case of human beings, the main channel for entry of Prana into our systems is breath; while the other four elements play subsidiary roles. In a similar way for the food we consume, *Prana* is assimilated through air, water, sunshine etc. This being so, fresh air, plentiful sunshine and pure water, enhances the life-force in any food derived from plant or animal sources. As a corollary, food produced with polluted inputs of any kind, are unable to give us the kind of *Prana* we need to live in a healthy and happy manner.

14

Other factors also contribute significantly to lowering the vital nutritive force in the food we consume. The processing of food is a major factor in this regard. With profit generally being the driving force behind any activity related to food production today, the loss of vitality in food can occur at any stage. The use of chemical fertilisers, the lure of premature harvesting, transportation of food over thousands of miles, refrigeration and preservation in synthetic chemical compounds, all go a long way in reducing the beneficial effects of food. In our quest to get food to look better, keep longer and be more pest resistant, genetic engineering has also come into the picture. Thus, each time we opt for a pre-packaged food item, instead of fresh and organic food, we drastically reduce the beneficial element of *Prana* in our intake and load our bodies with more chemicals to flush out. While we cannot all grow our own food, or shift to lifestyles that include only organic and non-processed food, we can definitely bring greater balance to choosing what we eat and reduce those elements that are likely to do the greatest damage to our health.

Much of the food we consume today is mechanically prepared. We all know that machines can work efficiently and clinically to execute the steps they are programmed to do. They minimise cost and maximise profit, and so provide us with a seemingly better way of doing everything. While the mechanisation of many activities that are part of daily life has a limited or no negative impact on the quality of life, the preparation of food does not fall into that category. This is because putting together and consuming a meal is greatly influenced by the 'consciousness' element.

Most of us, at some point in time or other, will have noted the difference between the results of an activity we engage in 'mindfully', in contrast to those we do in a pre-occupied manner. Imagine then, the results of an entire series of actions that have only the most peripheral human contact. It is the human touch, the attitude and the intent; all 'subtle' ingredients that lead to a unique final product in any area of life, and nowhere is this more evident than in the culinary world. Many of us relish food cooked by our mothers, something we attribute to the love that goes into the dish.

Brought up as we are in an environment that gives greater weightage to 'tangible' inputs of any kind, we struggle to comprehend that the mental, emotional and spiritual state of the person preparing the food does indeed impact the end result, almost entirely. In fact, we are so embedded in the physical realm that while we seek to increasingly sanitise everything that comes into contact with our food, we ignore the intangibles totally. So while we take great pains to wash the visible dirt off vegetables, we ignore how the cook is feeling when preparing the food, thus losing out on the subtler kinds of *Prana* that would be automatically infused into food prepared with love and care. The need to adopt ways and means that can help counter this, gains urgency if we are to live healthier and happier lives. If we take the trouble to prepare our own food, this is one aspect that is well within our control and truly worthy of consideration.

Sattva, Rajas, Tamas & a *Sattvik* Diet

One of the major steps that can enhance the quality of our lives by increasing the *Prana* factor in our food, is embracing a *sattvik* diet. To understand what *sattvik* food is, we must go back to the Ayurvedic concepts and understand *Sattva*, *Rajas* and *Tamas* – the three *gunas* or qualities that are characteristics of *Prakriti* (manifested consciousness). *Sattva* is the quality of clarity and balance; *Rajas* is that of action and change; and *Tamas* is the

15

attribute of inertia. While all three *guna*s exist within and around us, it is the quality of *Sattva* that we should seek to most preserve in our lives since on the physical level, it is a *sattvik* system that is most resistant to disease and has the ability to continue a state of healthy balance, adapting when the need arises. Additionally, for those of us who wish to advance in a spiritual direction, it is the development of this *guna* that provides a launching pad.

So what is *Sattvik* food? Simply put, it is food that allows the body to stay in balance. In other words, food that provides the right amount of *Prana* and is easily digested, allowing the systems to function optimally. It is food that does not leave us feeling tired and sluggish (as *Tamasik* food does), or over-stimulated and restless (as *Rajasik* food does), but allows the body and mind to continue in a state of calm and energised clarity – a condition most of us have experienced only in brief moments. Imagine a state where sleep is easy and does not hover on the fringes of consciousness because of a hyperactive mind. Imagine also, a day without any feeling of sleep deficit or sluggishness – when the ability to focus is unimpeded and moods do not rule. We spend days just waiting to feel 'up to life'. While, through conscious management of our diet, there exists the possibility of virtually breezing through our days. The tool for this transformation is none other than the gradual but persistent effort to incorporate *Sattvik* food into our daily diet and doing away with excess of any kind.

The ground rules for keeping our food intake within the ambit of *Sattvik* food then, is to ensure that the ingredients are as fresh as possible; the use of spices is judicious and moderate; and that a minimal amount of heat is used in the cooking process. Where possible, be the cook. If not, consume the food after expressing inner gratitude for the nourishment that the meal provides you with and eat with complete awareness, and away from, distracting influences. A key factor to remember is that leftovers, a key ingredient of most daily menus, should be avoided. Even the most lovingly and carefully prepared food begins to change character with the passage of time and hence its life-enhancing properties are slowly lost.

A BALANCED DIET
Understanding the Effects of Common Foods

1. Oils, Fats & *Ghee*

The Sanskrit word *sneha*, ranges in meaning from love and affection to unctuous and oily. When the soul feels love, we are energized, uplifted and cherished. In a similar vein, oils and fats carry essential nutrients throughout our bodies, strengthening and nourishing muscles and tissues. Without love, life has a distinct dryness. Similarly, in the absence of oils and fats, our diet is incomplete. Banishing all oils from our food is detrimental to our health. The important thing is to choose wisely and consume in moderation, keeping in view your constitution type. *Vata* constitution can use relatively larger quantities, whether through internal consumption or massage etc, as compared to *Kapha* or *Pitta* types, who are advised to use oil sparingly. Some oils commonly used for cooking are:

- Canola oil : also known as rapeseed oil, similar to sunflower oil, and suitable for all body types.
- Coconut oil: more suitable for *Pitta* types, on account of its cooling properties.
- Corn oil: a light oil with a drying nature, hence more appropriate for *Kapha* body types; limited use by *Pitta* and *Vata*.
- Mustard oil: its heating properties make this oil suitable for *Kapha* constitutions. In cold climates this oil is especially recommended for massage purposes.
- Olive oil: extra-virgin varieties of the oil are well known to be beneficial for health and can be used in the form of salad dressings or for preparations of sauces that require little application of heat.
- Safflower oil: good for deep-frying.
- Sesame oil: this is a good cooking oil, especially for *Vata* types.
- Sunflower oil: cooling in nature and good for *Pitta* constitutions.

2. Herbs & Spices

Ayurvedic cooking appreciates the critical role played by taste (rasa) in the effective digestion and assimilation of food by the human body. Herbs and spices are thus key to getting the best out of the food we consume. They play this part by stimulating gastric nerves, leading to release of the required enzymes and proper digestion. Properties of some commonly used herbs and spices are discussed below.

- Ajwain: (carom seeds) stimulates digestion.
- Asafoetida: (hing) aids digestion of fats and lentils.
- Basil (Holy): an antiseptic which enhances the immune system.
- Cardamom: a digestive stimulant. It clarifies the mind and is best used raw.
- Chilli: works as a digestive stimulant, are heating and a source of Vitamin C – best avoided by Pitta constitutions.
- Cinnamon: enhances digestive ability and helps combat nausea.
- Clove: highly antiseptic, heating and works as an expectorant.
- Coriander: cooling, a diuretic, and aids in the assimilation of digested food.
- Cumin: helpful in digesting starch and cellulose, while reducing flatulence.
- Curry Leaves: works as a digestive stimulant, is cooling and an astringent. It acts as a blood purifier and liver tonic.
- Fennel: increases digestive fire without aggravating Pitta; increases clarity of mind and has an overall calming effect
- Fenugreek: improves glucose utilization by the body and is considered beneficial for those suffering from blood sugar problems. It also works as a mild laxative and expectorant.
- Ginger: is heating, anti-infectious and help to combat nausea.
- Mint: is anti-inflammatory, a digestive aid, an anti-spasmodic pain-reliever; remedies halitosis and helps fight nausea.
- Mustard: is anti-bacterial, anti-fungal (hence, often included in pickles).
- Nutmeg: works as a sedative, is heating, anti-inflammatory and a pain reliever.
- Pepper: works as a stimulant to the digestive and circulatory systems.
- Saffron: is a tonic for the heart, liver and nerves. Highly valued in Ayurveda for its ability to balance all three doshas.

18

- Tamarind: has a cooling effect and is and anti-infectious. Works as a mild laxative and digestive and balances Vata Dosha.
- Turmeric: is a potent liver detoxifier. It boosts the immune system and reduces cholesterol.

3. **Milk & Milk Products**

- *Ghee*: though produced by heating butter, *ghee* differs in its remarkable properties. While butter can clog, *ghee* can free up passage ways. In Ayurveda, *ghee* is considered an essential of human diet as it stimulates the movement of bodily fluids and enhances the production of digestive juices and enzymes.
- Milk: one of the first foods identified in the *Veda*s. Pure milk, drawn from healthy cows, is a natural *Sattvik* food. Boiling milk with some ginger, cardamom, saffron, freshly ground black pepper or *tulsi*, allows it to be digested and eliminated easily. Ayurveda advises that milk is best consumed by itself or combined with dried or cooked fruits. Milk should never have salt added to it or be combined with vegetables, fish or meat. *Kapha* constitutions should avoid buffalo or cow's milk and go in for goat's milk instead. One glass of milk a day is sufficient for *Pitta* and *Vata* types of constitutions.
- Yoghurt: (fresh *dahi* or *thayir*) is alkaline and an easily digestible substance. It turns acidic as it sours and can aggravate *Pitta*. As an accompaniment to meals, it triggers the digestive process of more complex foods. It benefits the intestinal tract by helping to eliminate harmful bacteria while encouraging the beneficial *lactobacillus* variety. Sweetened yoghurt is advised for *Pitta*, spiced yoghurt for *Vata*, and yoghurt with the addition of herbs, for *Kapha*.
- *Paneer*: (fresh cottage cheese) is common in north India and is easier to digest than fermented cheeses. It is considered a good source of protein and calcium for *Vata* and *Kapha* constitutions.

19

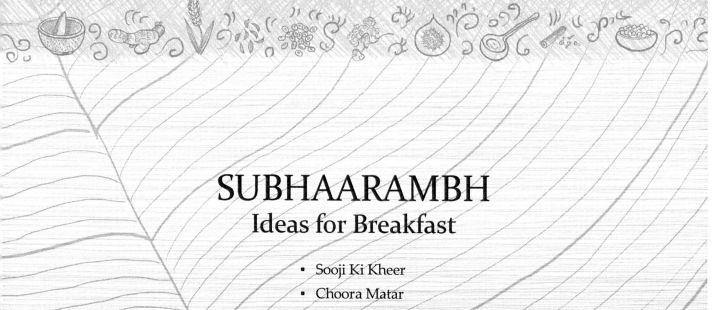

SUBHAARAMBH
Ideas for Breakfast

- Sooji Ki Kheer
- Choora Matar
- Sookhi Chhunki Moong ki Dal
- Upma
- Dalia
- Besan aur Lauki ka Chila
- Idli
- Dosa
- Uttapam
- Adai

Sooji ki Kheer
Sweet Semolina Porridge

This dish is quick and simple to prepare and easy to digest. Most children growing up in India identify beaten rice or poha, with the story of Lord Krishna and Sudama. To recount: Krishna and Sudama went their different ways after finishing their studies at the ashram of Rishi Sandeepani. While Krishna ruled Dwarka, Sudama lived the austere life of a simple brahmin. *As time passed, Sudama and his wife found it difficult to provide adequate food, clothing and shelter for their children, given their meagre resources.*

Remembering the deep friendship Sudama had shared with Lord Krishna, Sudama's wife persuaded him to go to him and seek help. Not wishing to meet his old friend empty-handed, Sudama took along some borrowed poha as a token gift.

The two friends met warmly and Sudama was treated as an honoured guest by Krishna and his wife, Rukmini. Seeing the riches and splendour that surrounded Krishna in the palace, Sudama hesitated and withheld the gift of poha till the Lord himself took the cloth containing the beaten rice and ate the poha with relish. Sudama was so overjoyed to meet his childhood friend that he forgot to ask for any material help for himself or his family and only remembered his omission later. However, to his great surprise, on his return, he found his hut had been transformed into a palacial dwelling and his family living in the lap of luxury.

It is said that the meeting between Krishna and Sudama took place on Akshaya Tritiya.

21

INGREDIENTS
¼ cup (50 gms) semolina (*sooji/rava*)
1 tbsp clarified butter (*ghee*)
2½ cups (500 ml) milk, preboiled (*dudh*)
1/5 cup (40 gms) sugar (*sakkar*)
A pinch of cardamom powder (*ilaichi*)
10-15 raisins (*kishmish*)

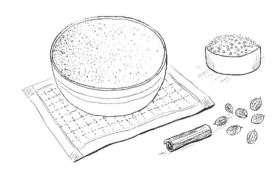

METHOD

1. Heat a pan or *kadhai* on medium heat for 2 minutes. Then put in the *ghee*. Once the *ghee* has heated, add the *sooji* and roast on low to medium heat, stirring gently, till it turns a pinkish-brown colour. Pay close attention while doing this because the *sooji* can burn easily. When done, the *sooji* will emit an appetizing aroma. Remove from heat and allow to cool.
2. Once cool, add the milk, stirring constantly to avoid formation of lumps. Place the pan back on heat. Cook for another 5 minutes, stirring all the while. The *sooji* will swell and the mixture will thicken to the consistency of porridge as it cooks.
3. Add the sugar and mix well.
4. Sprinkle a pinch of cardamom powder.
5. Garnish with the raisins and finely sliced almonds. *Sooji ki Kheer* is ready to serve.

NOTES

✓ For a *kapha* constitution, pre-boil the milk with cardamom and ginger before using it for this dish.
✓ Raw or unrefined sugar can also be used as a sweetening agent

CHOORA MATAR
Beaten Rice Flakes with Green Peas

The word gram, *is commonly used in India for pulses/lentils. This came from the Portuguese word,* grao, *which indicated all types of grains. It is first believed to have been used for* chana dal *or Bengal gram, before spreading to include the other varieties of* dals.

INGREDIENTS
2 cups beaten rice (*poha/ chura*)
1½ cups green peas, fresh or frozen (*matar*)
2-3 tbsp finely chopped ginger (*adrak*)
2-3 green chillies, finely chopped (*hari mirch*)
3-4 tbsp finely chopped fresh coriander (*dhania patta*)
2 tbsp mango powder (*amchur*)
2 tbsp *garam masala*
Salt to taste (*namak*)
2 tsp lemon juice (*limbu*)
1 tbsp oil (*tel*)

23

METHOD
1. Heat oil in a *kadhai* or fry pan. Add the green chillies and ginger and fry for a minute before adding the peas. Cover and cook on low heat till the peas are done.
2. Meanwhile, lightly sprinkle the *poha* with water, making it slightly damp. Take care not to use excess water, otherwise lumps may form. Once the *poha* is moist, add the coriander powder, *amchur* and *garam masala*. Mix with a light hand adding salt to taste.
3. Once the peas are done, mix the *poha* in and heat, stirring carefully till heated through. Cover and cook for a minute to allow the steam to help the *poha* absorb the flavours. Turn off the heat. Add the lime juice and garnish with chopped coriander before serving.

SOOKHI CHHUNKI MOONG KI DAL
Dry Tempered Yellow Mung Beans

Bhima, the second of the Pandava princes, was also called Vrikodara, *meaning 'wolf-belly' and 'one who has the fire* Vrika *in his stomach'. When food was cooked in the Pandava home, half was put aside for Bhima while the rest of the family consumed the remaining portion.*

INGREDIENTS

1 cup split & de-husked mung beans (*moong dal*)

¼ tsp turmeric powder (*haldi*)

½ tsp cumin seeds (*jeera*)

A pinch of asafoetida (*hing*)

1 tbsp grated ginger (*adrak*)

1 tbsp finely chopped green chillies (*hari mirch*)

1 tbsp lemon juice (*limbu*)

2 tbsp chopped coriander leaves (*dhania patta*)

Salt to taste (*namak*)

1 tbsp oil (*tel*)

24

METHOD

1. Wash the *dal*. Put in a frying pan, add the turmeric and salt and cook in just enough water to make it soft but not mushy.
2. Heat the oil in a separate pan and add the cumin seeds. Once they splutter, add the asafoetida, ginger and green chillies. Stir fry for about a minute. Add the cooked *dal* to this tempering and gently mix, taking care not to crush the *dal*. Add more salt if needed. Take off the heat and add lemon juice. Mix well. Garnish with chopped coriander and serve.

NOTES

✓ Adjust the quantity of ginger and green chillies depending on their potency. Ginger becomes stronger as it ages, so use more if it is really fresh.

✓ Avoid pre-soaking the *dal* since moong cooks easily and can turn mushy.

UPMA
Savoury Semolina Crumble

Navadhanya *are the nine grains offered to the* Navagraha*s (Nine Planets), as part of* pujas *and rituals: i. Bengal Gram* (chana)*: Brihaspati; ii. Wheat* (gehun)*: Surya; iii. Horse Gram* (kulthi)*: Ketu; iv. Green Gram* (moong)*: Buddh; v. Rice: Chandra; vi. White Beans: Shukra; vii. Black Sesame Seeds: Shani; viii. Black Gram* (urad)*: Rah; and ix. Chickpeas: Mangal*

INGREDIENTS

2 cups semolina (*sooji*)
1 carrot, finely chopped or grated (*gajar*)
½ cup chopped French beans (*fansi*)
2 tsp chopped green chillies (*hari mirch*)
2 tsp chopped ginger (*adrak*)
½ tsp mustard seeds (*rai*)
6-8 curry leaves (*kari patta*)
2 tbsp chopped coriander (*dhania patta*)
Salt to taste (*namak*)
4 cups water

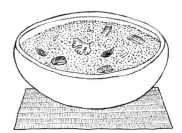

25

METHOD
1. Heat a pan or *kadhai* on medium heat for 2 minutes and put in the *sooji*. Roast on low to medium heat, stirring gently till it turns pinkish-brown and emits a pleasing aroma.
2. In another pan, heat the oil and add the mustard seeds. Once they splutter, add the curry leaves, followed by the ginger and green chillies. Stir for a few seconds.
3. Add the carrots and French beans and sauté till done.
4. Add salt and water and bring to a boil. Once the water has come to a rolling boil, add the *sooji* slowly, stirring all the while to make sure no lumps form. Once all the *sooji* is incorporated, stir the mixture well. Lower the heat and cook for another couple of minutes. Serve hot, garnished with fresh, chopped coriander.

NOTES
✓ The *sooji* can be roasted in a tablespoon of *ghee* to give a better taste and aroma
✓ Green peas (fresh or frozen), are often added to *upma,* as also chopped tomatoes.
✓ The beans and carrots can be blanched first, to reduce cooking time.

DALIA
Savoury Broken Wheat Crumble

INGREDIENTS

1 cup broken wheat (*dalia*)
2 tbsp oil (*tel*)
¼ cup finely chopped French beans (fansi)
¼ cup finely chopped carrot (*gajar*)
¼ cup finely chopped capsicum (*capsi*)
½ tsp cumin seeds (*jeera*)
½ tsp crushed black pepper (*kala mirch*)
Salt to taste (*namak*)
2 tsp lemon juice (*limbu*)
2 tbsp finely chopped fresh coriander (*dhania patta*)

26

METHOD

1. Dry roast the broken wheat in a pan on medium heat.
2. In a pressure cooker, add the broken wheat with twice the quantity of water and pressure cook for 2 whistles. Set aside. Once the pressure has released, check if the *dalia* is done. Drain any excess water (preserve this to cooking the vegetables)
3. In a frying pan or *kadhai*, heat the oil and add the cumin seeds. Once they crackle, add the crushed black pepper and chopped vegetables and stir fry for two mins. Add salt, 2 tbsp water. Cover and cook on low heat for 5 mins. When the vegetables are done, add the cooked *dalia* and lemon juice. Mix well with a light hand. Garnish with chopped coriander and serve hot.

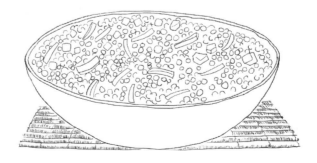

BESAN AUR LAUKI KA CHILA
Gram Flour & Bottle Gourd Crépes

The Taittiriya Upanishad *describes the five sheaths/layers that comprise all living entities, from the outer to the innermost as follows:* Annamaya Kosha: *sustained by food;* Pranamaya Kosha: *sustained by energy;* Manomaya Kosha: *sustained by the mind;* Vijnanamaya Kosha: *sustained by the intellect;* Anandamaya Kosha: *sustained by bliss. Of these, the* Annamaya Kosha *corresponds to the physical body* (Sthula sharira); *the* Pranamaya, Manomaya *and* Vijnanamaya koshas *to the subtle body* (sukshma sharira), *and the* Anandamaya kosha *to the causal body* (karana sharira). *The starting point for any self-transformation therefore, has to be the* Annamaya Kosha.

INGREDIENTS
2 cups chickpea flour (*besan*)
2/3 cup grated bottle gourd (*lauki*)
½ tsp carom seeds (*ajwain*)
A pinch of red chilli powder (*lal mirch*)
Water
Salt to taste (*namak*)
A pinch of soda bi carb
Oil for shallow frying (*tel*)

METHOD
1. Squeeze the excess water from the grated bottle gourd. Preserve the water.
2. In a mixing bowl, put in the *besan* and add in all the dry ingredients (salt, red chilli powder and soda bi carb). Mix well.
3. Add the grated *lauki* and then the preserved water. The batter should be thick and gooey at this point. Add more water to bring it to a pouring consistency.
4. Heat a frying pan and pour the prepared batter. Spread evenly using a ladle.
5. Add a few drops of oil on each side of the *chila*. Cook on medium heat till the edges begin to leave the sides of the pan and the *chila* turns golden brown.
6. Serve with green chutney and *rasedar alu ki sabzi*.

NOTE
✓ Adding *lauki* gives a softer texture to the *chila*. Other vegetables like carrots can also be grated and added to the batter.

IDLI
Steamed Rice Flour Cakes

Regional variations of dosa *recipes are found all across peninsular India. It finds mention in Sangam litera-ture. King Someshwara of Kalyana, wrote* Manasollasa, *in about 1130 AD, where the preparation of food, especially in royal kitchens, was discussed. It is among the first works that mentions food items like* idli, dosa, shrikhand, pheni, laddoos *etc., and gives recipes. The 17th century Tamil work,* Maccapuranam, *mentions the* ittali, *whereas in Kannada literature,* iddaliga *is a steamed food made only with* urad dal batter.

INGREDIENTS

3 cups boiled rice (*ukhada chawal*)
1 cup husked black beans (*chilka urad dal*)
1 tsp salt (*namak*)
¼ tsp fenugreek seeds (*dhania patta*)
1/3 cup leftover cooked rice (*chawal*)

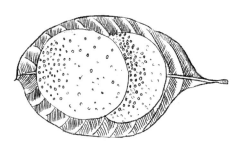

METHOD
For the Batter
1. Soak the rice and *urad dal* separately for 6-8 hours. Drain the water into a separate bowl. Use this to add in the grinding process if needed.
2. Grind the *dal* with the *methi* seeds till light and fluffy, adding water if needed.
3. In the same mixer-grinder jar, grind the rice till it reaches a grainy consistency. Add the cooked rice and blend well.
4. Mix the rice and *dal* batter adding salt.Leave the batter to ferment overnight.

For the *Idlis*
1. Next morning, stir the batter well. The aroma will tell you if it has fermented.
2. Grease the *idli* moulds well (not if you are using non-stick idli moulds) and pour in the batter till just below the edge of the moulds.
3. Pour some water into the *idli* steamer/ pressure cooker, taking care that it does not touch the bottom of the lower-most *idli* moulds. Bring to a boil and lower in the *idli* moulds. Close the lid and steam for 12-15 minutes.

28

4. Remove from the steamer and check if the *idli*s are done by piercing one with a tooth-pick/ fork – it should come out clean.
5. Cool for 5 minutes. Remove from the moulds and serve with sambhar and coconut chutney.

NOTES

✓ The proportion of boiled rice to *urad dal* varies from household to household, with some recipes using almost six times the amount of rice to the *dal*.
✓ Adding either leftover cooked rice or beaten rice soaked in yoghurt, is said to aid the fermentation process. It also adds to the softness of the *idli*s.
✓ In cold weather, allow more time for fermentation or place the batter in a warm place (can be kept in an oven pre-heated to 200 F and then turned off).

29

DOSA
Rice-Lentil Crepés with Fermented Batter

INGREDIENTS

4 cups boiled rice (*ukhada chawal*)
1 cups black beans (*urad dal*)
½ tsp fenugreek seeds (*methi dana*)
Salt to taste (*namak*)

METHOD
For the Batter
1. Soak the rice and *dal* separately for 6-8 hours, adding the fenugreek seeds to the *dal* while it soaks.
2. Grind the *dal* (with fenugreek seeds) till smooth and remove into a mixing bowl.
3. Grind the soaked rice till it is fine but grainy (the rice should always have a hint of graininess).
4. Mix the ground rice with the *dal* and leave to ferment overnight (as for *idli*).

For the *Dosa*s
1. Heat a griddle or if using a regular *tava*, cut an onion in half and smear oil on the griddle using the flat surface of the onion to do so – this makes the batter less likely to stick to the griddle.
2. Pour some batter onto the hot griddle and use the ladle to quickly spread it in a spiralling clockwise motion.
3. Add a few drops of oil to the edges of the *dosa* and on it as well. Cook on medium heat. Once the batter leaves the sides and the *dosa* turns golden, flip and let the other side cook for a few seconds.
4. Cook all the *dosa*s in the same way. Serve hot with *sambhar* and chutney.

UTTAPAM
Rice-Lentil Pancakes with Fermented Batter

The cooking area in Indian homes was always regarded as a special and sacred place. This was because it was not seen merely as where food was prepared but as an environment that facilitated the strengthening of the connection between man and the cosmos. Cooking was not a process that assuaged just physical hunger, it was the recharging of the body and mind on a far greater scale. For this reason, food was never to be eaten standing up, moving about or in the midst of any other distraction (like watching TV), but while sitting down in silence.

INGREDIENTS

2 cups *dosa* batter (refer *Dosa* recipe)
1 medium-sized tomato, finely chopped (*tamatar*)
1 green chilli, finely chopped (*hari mirch*)
½ cup finely chopped fresh coriander (*dhania patta*)

32

METHOD

1. Heat a griddle or *tava*, as for *dosa*. Spread the batter in a thick layer and sprinkle the chopped tomatoes, green chillies and coriander on the *uttapam*. When one side seems done, flip over. Allow the onion garnish to cook for half a minute before taking it off the pan.
2. Serve hot with chutney and *sambhar*.

NOTE

✓ The tomatoes, green chillies and coriander, can also be mixed into the batter if time is short.

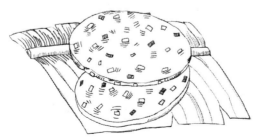

ADAI
Rice-Lentil Pancakes with Fresh Batter

INGREDIENTS

1 cup rice (*chawal*)

½ cup pigeon peas (*tur dal*)

¼ cup husked black beans (*urad dal*)

2-3 whole dried red chillies (*Kashmiri mirch*) OR
   10-15 whole black peppercorns (*sabut kala mirch*)

¼ tsp asafoetida powder (*hing*)

1 medium-sized carrot, chopped (*gajar*)

1 medium-sized onion, chopped fine (*pyaaz*)

2 tbsp chopped fresh coriander (*dhania patta*)

7-8 curry leaves (*kari patta*)

3-4 tbsp oil (*tel*)

Salt to taste (*namak*)

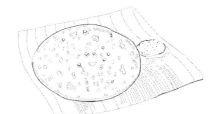

33

METHOD

1. Soak the rice and lentils for half an hour. Drain the water.
2. In a grinder, blend the rice and lentils with the red chillies, asafoetida and salt, into a coarse batter. Add the chopped vegetables and curry leaves to the paste.
3. Heat a *tava* or griddle (if using a regular *tava*, cut an onion in half and smear oil on the griddle using the flat surface of the onion – this makes the batter less likely to stick to the griddle).
4. Pour a ladleful of batter on the hot *tava* and in quick spiralling motions, spread from the centre to the outside (as for *dosas*). Drizzle drops of oil around the edges of the *adai* and in the centre. Once the bottom turns golden brown, flip onto the other side and cook for half a minute.
5. Serve hot with coconut chutney.

BEVERAGES & SOUPS

The Kanchipuram temple precincts contain a famous mango tree – the four branches of which bear fruit with distinctly different tastes and flavours. The tree is thought to be over 3000 years old and each branch is said to represent one of the four Vedas. According to Ayurveda, the sweeter the mango – the more easily digested it is.

- Aam ka Panha
- Thandai
- Sweet Lassi
- Chhaas
- Adrak ki Chai
- Kokum Sharbat
- Mixed Dal Soup
- Pepper Rasam
- Mugda Supa (Moong Soup)
- Detoxifying Brew

AAM KA PANHA
Raw Mango Refresher

Kalpavriksha – *the* samudra manthan (churning of the ocean), *brought many rare and precious objects to the world – among them was the wish-fulfilling tree, Kalpavrikhsa. Many varieties of trees are identified with this name today, including Coconut, Parijat and Banyan trees.*

INGREDIENTS

2 medium-sized green, unripe mangoes (*kachcha aam/ keri*)
2 cups water (1 to boil & 1 to blend with)
1-2 tsp black rock salt (*sendha namak*)
Sugar to taste (*sakkar*)
1 tsp cumin seeds, roasted & powdered (*jeera*)
2 fresh mint sprigs (*pudina*)

35

METHOD

1. Boil the mangoes till they are soft and the skin has split.
2. Cool, peel and mash the pulp. Discard the seeds.
3. In a blender, whiz the mango pulp with water, till a smooth purée has formed.
4. Depending on the sourness of the mangoes, spoon 2-3 tbsp of this purée into each tall glass and dissolve with cold water. Add sugar to taste, a pinch of rock salt and cumin powder. Mix well.
5. Serve cold, garnished with a sprig of mint.

NOTES

✓ In very hot weather, add 10-12 fresh mint leaves while blending the mango pulp.
✓ This thick purée can also be used as a chutney to accompany meals.

THANDAI
Spicy Almond & Poppy Seed Drink

A saint who wandered from village to village, was much loved for his wisdom. During the course of his travels, he was offered hospitality by the people he met, but he generally declined, preferring to rest beneath the open sky and cook his own food. It so happened that a devotee once refused to take no for an answer and the saint agreed to stay with him. After the meal, the saint and his host retired to their respective chambers for the night.

When he arose at his usual hour, the monk found himself unusually attracted by the sound of a sweet bell. The pattern of the chimes indicated that it was tied to the neck of an animal. Finding himself unable to meditate, the monk tiptoed his way towards the sound and on reaching the cowshed, saw that the bell hung around the neck of a cow. He swiftly untied it and rushed back to his room, where minutes later, he felt awash with remorse at his action.

Try as he might, he could not ascertain the reason for the aberration in his behaviour. The only deviation in his routine had been the acceptance of the merchant's hospitality.

The next day, he tactfully enquired about the cooking arrangements in his host's home and found that the lady of the house was well known for her avaricious nature. He at once realized that the food consumed by him the night before had carried the vibrations of her nature and affected him as well.

While we may feel that we are not affected in this way by the food we eat, in truth, the origin, manner of procurement, and preparation of the food, all carry subtle vibrations that can either increase or decrease our balance in life. It is for this reason that the food cooked by oneself at home, is held to be the most beneficial and eating out is discouraged.

INGREDIENTS
¾ cups almonds (*badam*)
1½ tsp peppercorns (*kala mirch*)
3-4 tbsp fennel seeds (*saunf*)
2-3 tsp musk melon seeds (*kharbooze ke beej/ magaz*)
2 tbsp dried rose petals (*gulab patta*)
2 cups water
3½ cups milk (*dudh*)
Sugar to taste (*sakkar*)
Crushed ice (*baraf*)

METHOD
1. In a mixer-grinder, grind the first four ingredients with half the milk, till a paste has formed.
2. Strain the paste through a sieve or muslin cloth.
3. Blend the solid paste thus obtained, with the remaining milk and sieve again.
4. Add the sugar and water to the resulting liquid, top with crushed ice, and serve in tall glasses.

37

SWEET LASSI
Sweet Yoghurt Cooler

According to Ayurveda, milk from a goat or cow is lighter and more easily digested than buffalo milk, which is heavier and colder (ie. more Kapha producing).

INGREDIENTS

2 cups plain yoghurt (*dahi*)
¼ cup milk (*dudh*)
4-6 tbsp sugar (*sakkar*)
¾ cup crushed ice (*baraf*)
2 sprigs of fresh mint (*pudina*)

METHOD

1. In a blender, add all the ingredients with ½ cup of crushed ice. Whiz till smooth and creamy.
2. Top with the remaining crushed ice and a sprig of mint and serve in tall glasses.

NOTES

✓ Plain *lassi* can be flavoured with different fruits to make fruit *lassi*. 1 cup of freshly diced mango, banana or strawberry works well for this.
✓ Using unrefined sugar will make the beverage healthier.
✓ Plain *lassi* can also be flavoured with rosewater (about 2 tbsp), to make it more cooling in hot weather.

CHHAAS
Spicy Yoghurt Beverage

Properties of common and uncommon juices:
Watermelon – effective diuretic
Lemon – appetite stimulant; antiseptic
Carrot – benefits the liver
Apple – good for the liver
Wheatgrass – effective cleanser
Blueberry and Cranberry – effective in prevention
 of urinary tract infections
Cabbage – ulcer healing properties
Red Cabbage – for chronic cough or asthma

INGREDIENTS
2 cups plain yoghurt (*dahi*)
½ tsp black rock salt (*sendha namak*)
Salt to taste (*namak*)
4-6 mint leaves (*pudina*)
2 tsp grated ginger (*adrak*)
1 green chilli, deseeded (*hari mirch*)
15-20 coriander leaves (*dhania patta*)
½ cup water

39

METHOD
1. Mix all ingredients, except the water, in a blender and whiz together till smooth.
2. Mix in the water to get the desired consistency and adjust salt as needed.
3. Serve chilled in tall glasses.

NOTE
✓ Add a pinch of asafoetida and a few curry leaves for a change of taste.

ADRAK KI CHAI
Fresh Ginger Tea with Milk

*Storing drinking water in a copper vessel was recommended by Ayurveda because of the germicidal proper-
ties of copper. Wandering yogis would inevitably carry a copper vessel (kamandalu) to store/drink water.
The ancient Egyptians also followed the practice of storing water in copper containers.*

INGREDIENTS

4 cups water
2 tsp tea leaves (*chai ki patti*)
2-3 tbsp fresh, grated ginger (*adrak*)
4-5 tsp milk, for light tea/3 tbsp for strong tea (*dudh*)
Sugar to taste (*sakkar*)

METHOD

40

1. Put the water and ginger into a saucepan and bring to a boil. Let it simmer for a couple
    of minutes before adding the milk, to allow the flavor of the ginger to infuse. Add the
    tea-leaves and stir.
2. For light ginger tea, take the pan off heat and rest for 1-2 minutes before straining the
    tea into individual cups and adding sugar as per taste.
3. For stronger tea, increase the quantity of milk and simmer on heat for 3 minutes.

NOTES

✓ For cardamom-flavoured tea, add 1 crushed pod of green cardamom per cup of tea
  and proceed as for ginger tea.
✓ The flavours of ginger, cardamom and clove can be combined to make *masala* tea when
  greater warmth is needed.
✓ Holy Basil (*tulsi*) is also a wonderful addition to this tea.

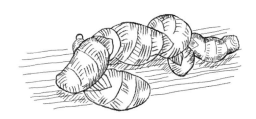

KOKUM SHARBAT
Sweet & Sour Refresher

INGREDIENTS

125-150 gms dried Garciana Indica (*kokum*)
6 cups water
Salt to taste (*namak*)
2 tsp black rock salt (*sendha namak*)
2 tsp cumin seeds, roasted & powdered (*jeera*)
Sugar to taste (*sakkar*)
6-8 mint leaves (*pudina*)

METHOD

1. Heat 2 cups of water and soak the *kokum* for 5-10 minutes.
2. Squeeze the pulp and strain.
3. In a blender, whiz the pulp and the roasted cumin powder with the remaining water.
4. Add salt, black rock salt and sugar to taste.
5. Garnish with mint leaves and serve chilled.

41

NOTES

✓ Crushed black pepper can be added to the *sharbat* for extra zing.
✓ *Kokum* is popular on the west coast of India and is widely used for its cooling and anti-oxidant properties. It is also a digestive tonic.
✓ *Kokum* can also be blended with coconut milk, green chillies and coriander to make a tasty accompaniment to meals in the summer months – this preparation is called *Sol Kadi* in Maharashtra.

MIXED DAL SOUP
Mixed Lentil Broth

Mulligatawny soup, popular with the Europeans during their sojourn in India, derives its name from millagu *(pepper) and* tanni *(water), the main ingredients to make 'pepper-water' or* rasam.

INGREDIENTS

2 level tbsp horse gram (*gahat/ muthira/ kulthi*)
1 level tbsp black gram (*urad*)
1 level tbsp green gram (*moong*)
1 level tbsp pigeon peas (*tuvar*)
¼ spoon crushed black pepper (*kali mirch*)
¼ spoon cumin seeds powder (*jeera*)
¼ spoon coriander powder (*dhania*)
¼ spoon dry ginger power (*adrak*)
Rock salt to taste (*sendha namak*)
2 cups water

42

METHOD

1. Clean the legumes well and soak them for 3 hours. Cook them until soft.
2. When done, purée them in a blender. Mix in the ground spices and salt. Add more water to adjust the consistency if needed. Simmer gently for 2-3 minutes.
3. Serve hot.

NOTES

✓ This soup balances all three *dosha*s
✓ A pinch of *pippali* (Indian long pepper) powder can be added to enhance the beneficial properties.

Mulligatawny Soup

PEPPER RASAM
Peppercorn Broth

Vedic literature refers to the 3Ms – the trio of lentils comprising, Masha (Urad, *Black gram*), Mudga (Moong, *Green gram*) *and* Masura (Masoor, *Brown lentil*). *Tuvar or* Arhar (Pigeon peas) *is a relatively later member of the family of lentils popular throughout India.*

Moong *flour or powder is a gentle and effective cleanser for the skin and hair while* Masoor *flour is particularly effective for clearing skin blemishes.*

INGREDIENTS
1-2 tbsp thick tamarind pulp (*imli*)
2½ cups water
Salt to taste (*namak*)
10-12 peppercorns (*sabut kala mirch*)
1 tsp cumin seeds (*jeera*)
8-10 curry leaves (*kari patta*)
2 tbsp chopped fresh coriander (*dhania patta*)
¼ tsp mustard seeds (*rai*)
1 tsp clarified butter (*ghee*)

44

METHOD
1. Simmer the tamarind pulp with salt in 2 cups of water for about 5 minutes.
2. Powder the curry leaves, peppercorns and cumin seeds coarsely.
3. In a frying pan, heat the *ghee* and add the mustard seeds. Once these pop, add the tamarind broth and ground spices. Add more water if needed and adjust the salt.
4. Garnish with chopped coriander and serve hot.

MUGDA SUPA
Mung Beans Soup

INGREDIENTS

1 cup green gram (*moong*)
3 cups water
¼ spoon pepper powder (*kali mirch*)
¼ spoon long pepper powder (*pippali*)
¼ spoon cumin seeds powder (*jeera*)
¼ spoon coriander powder (*dhania*)
¼ spoon dry ginger power (*adrak*)
Rock salt to taste (*sendha namak*)

METHOD

1. Soak the green gram for 3 hours. Cook it in sufficient water until it becomes soft.
2. Add pepper powder, coriander powder, cumin seeds powder, long pepper powder, dry ginger power and rock salt. Mix well.
3. Serve hot and enjoy your soup.

NOTES

✓ In Ayurveda, this soup is said to be the best among wholesome diets.
✓ It balances the three *dosha*s.
✓ It improves taste and appetite.
✓ It is given for those who have undergone detoxification therapy in Ayurveda.
✓ It is nourishing and strengthening.
✓ It induces sweating.
✓ It relieves diseases of the throat and eyes.
✓ It relieves internal and external ulcers.

DETOXIFYING BREW

The cow has always been regarded as sacred in India. According to the **Srimad Bhagavatam**, *during the reign of King Prithu, there once occurred a terrible famine. All living creatures faced unending misery with the earth unable to produce sustenance. Meditating on the problem, the King had a vision of Mother Earth in the form of a cow. She explained to him that all sustenance required for living creatures would be provided by the planet and this would be diverse enough to suit the different needs of people and animals living in varying climatic conditions. What would be required from mankind, would be the effort to produce the food following the laws of the natural world. It is said that following the vision, the King worked along with his subjects to ensure prosperity and plentitude.*

INGREDIENTS
¼ tsp cumin seeds (*jeera*)
½ tsp fennel seeds (*sauf*)
½ tsp coriander seeds (*dhanadal*)

46

METHOD
1. Boil 500 ml of water and add the spices. Cover and let it steep for 15 mins before straining the infusion.
2. Sip throughout the day.

NOTE
✓ Store the liquid in a thermos flask to maintain the temperature.

SALADS & SNACKS

- Moong-Anardana Salad
- Makkai aur Capsicum Salad
- Kale Chane ki Chat
- Paneer Pakora
- Palak Pakora
- Bhelpuri
- Kosambari
- Kabuli Chana Sundal

MOONG-ANARDANA SALAD
Mung Beans & Pomegranate Salad

INGREDIENTS

1½ cups whole mung beans (*moong*)
2 cups pomegranate seeds (*anardana*)
A pinch of black rock salt (*sendha namak*)
½ tsp cumin seeds, roasted & powdered (*jeera*)
¼ tsp dried & powdered ginger (*adrak*)
1 tsp oil (*tel*)

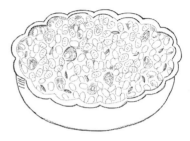

METHOD

1. Soak the *moong dal* for 4-6 hours. Steam cook till tender.
2. Heat oil in a frying pan and add the *moong. S*tir-fry for 2-3 minutes. Remove from heat and remove into a serving bowl.
3. Mix together with the pomegranate seeds and spices and serve.

NOTES

✓ Ayurveda considers raw salads difficult to digest and recommends that they be eaten lightly cooked and as part of the mid-day meal.
✓ *Moong* is considered to be the most easily digested of all lentils. This salad can also be made with sprouted *moong*.
✓ The addition of cumin and ginger counteracts gas, which some people experience on consuming lentils. The black rock salt goes well with the taste of pomegranate.

Makkai aur Capsicum Salad
Corn & Bell Pepper Salad

It is said that of the four teertha dhams, *Lord Vishnu bathes at Rameswaram, meditates at Badrinath, dines at Puri, and rests at Dwarka. Accordingly, the preparation of food at the Jagannath Puri temple is a truly sacred and elaborate affair. The* mahaprasad *cooked there is treated as* Anna Brahma *and is prepared in clay utensils by 400 cooks on 752 wood fired sigris. Chhapan bhog (five types of offering), is prepared every day and the temple is said to have the largest kitchen in the world.*

INGREDIENTS
1 cup corn kernels, boiled
1 cup deseeded & chopped bell peppers
1 cup peeled, deseeded & chopped cucumber
¼ tsp rock salt (
1 tsp lemon juice (limbu)
1 tsp oil (tel)

49

METHOD
1. Heat oil in a pan, add the corn kernels, bell peppers and cucumber, and stir-fry for 2-3 minutes.
2. Remove from heat and add the rock salt and lemon juice.
3. Serve warm.

KALE CHANE KI CHAT
Spicy Black Chickpea Salad

INGREDIENTS

1 cup black Bengal gram, soaked overnight (*kala chana*)
3 medium-sized tomatoes, chopped fine (*tamatar*)
2 tbsp thinly sliced ginger (*adrak*)
1-2 finely chopped green chillies (*hari mirch*)
2-3 tbsp finely chopped fresh coriander (*dhania patta*)
1 tsp carom seeds (*ajwain*)
A pinch of asafoetida (*hing*)
Salt to taste (*namak*)
1 tbsp oil (*tel*)

50

METHOD

1. Boil the *kala chana* which has been soaked overnight, in a pressure cooker with a pinch of salt, till it is tender. Drain and set aside.
2. In a frying pan or *kadhai*, heat the oil and add the *ajwain*, followed by the asafoetida. Once the seeds pop, put in the green chillies and ginger and stir-fry for 2-3 minutes.
3. Add the chopped tomatoes, cover and cook till done.
4. Put in the drained *kala chana* and mix well.
5. Garnish with chopped coriander and serve warm.

NOTES

✓ This snack/salad can be tempered with cumin seeds instead of *ajwain* for a change of taste.
✓ The addition of fresh crumbled *paneer* (cottage cheese), with a dash of lemon juice and a sprinkling of *chaat masala*, will make this into a more filling snack.

PANEER PAKORA
Indian Cottage Cheese Fritters

The food options we exercise can help us acclimatize to new surroundings and cope better with seasonal changes. In cold and dry climates (Vata aggravating), modify the diet to include more liquid, oils and fats (through oil massages too). When the weather is humid, include more drying and cooling foods to counter the heat. As a general rule, inhabitants of busy towns and cities are likely to suffer from increased Vata and Pitta. The nature of your individual constitution remains fundamental to the choices you make.

INGREDIENTS

400 gms cottage cheese, cut into 2″ cubes (*paneer*)
1½ cups gram flour (*besan*)
½ cup rice flour (*akiki*)
Salt to taste (*namak*)
½ tsp red chilli powder (*lal mirch powder*)
½ tsp cumin seeds (*jeera*) OR ½ tsp carom seeds (*ajwain*)
A pinch of turmeric powder (*haldi*)
Water as required

51

METHOD

1. Mix the *besan* and rice flour with the ground spices and cumin/carom seeds. Add water to make a batter of coating consistency. Add salt to taste. Set aside.
2. Heat oil in a deep frying pan/*kadhai*. To test for the correct temperature, drop some batter into the oil – if it rises quickly to the surface, the oil is ready.
3. Dip the *paneer* pieces in the batter to coat them well and fry them in the hot oil till they are golden brown.
4. Remove from the oil and drain well.
5. Serve hot with green chutney or tamarind chutney.

NOTES

✓ To make the batter more crisp, ½ tsp of baking soda can be added and mixed into the batter just before the paneer is dipped into it.
✓ In another option, club soda can be substituted in part in place of the water when preparing the batter.

PALAK PAKORA
Spinach Fritters

While the medicinal properties of onion and garlic have been well recognized by Ayurveda, both of these items do not find place in sattvik *food. This is because garlic increases* rajas, *while onion enhances* tamas *in the body and mind. In other words, they are likely to over-stimulate the central nervous system and slow down physical responses. Accordingly, they should be used sparingly, if at all, particularly by* Pitta *and* Kapha *constitutions respectively, and generally only to counter specific medical conditions.*

INGREDIENTS

15-20 medium-sized fresh spinach leaves (*palak*)

1 cup Bengal gram flour (*besan*)

1tbsp rice flour (*akiki*)

½ tsp turmeric (*haldi*)

½ tsp red chilli powder (*lal mirchi powder*)

½ tsp carom seeds (*ajwain*)

Salt to taste (*namak*)

Oil to deep fry (*tel*)

Water to make batter

Chaat masala for sprinkling

METHOD

1. Make a smooth batter of the *besan*, rice flour, turmeric, red chilli powder and carom seeds. Add salt to taste.
2. Wash and dry the spinach leaves and set aside.
3. In a *kadhai*/frying pan, heat the oil. To test for the correct temperature, drop some batter into the oil – if it rises quickly to the surface, the oil is ready.
4. Coat the spinach leaves with the batter one by one and deep fry till golden brown.
5. Remove the pakoras from the oil and drain well.
6. Sprinkle with *chat masala* and serve hot with green chutney or tamarind chutney.

NOTES

✓ Deep fried food is heavier on the stomach and should be consumed sparingly.

✓ The *pakoras* should be eaten hot and eating leftovers should be strictly avoided.

BHELPURI
Tangy Puffed-Rice Snack

Salt does not find mention in the Rig Veda and features only in the later Vedas. Ayurveda appreciates salt as an 'agni' and 'taste' enhancer and finds rock salt as the most beneficial among the different varieties though the ancient texts list upto nine varieties of salt. Salty taste comprises water and fire and hence excess salt will increase kapha and pitta because of which persons who are overweight and/or have high blood pressure are advised to strictly limit their salt intake. Canned foods generally contain fairly large amounts of salt and hence are avoidable.

INGREDIENTS

2 cups puffed rice (*murmura/ laiya/ kurmura*)
1 medium-sized potato, boiled, peeled & cubed (*alu*)
1 medium-sized cucumber, peeled & chopped (*kakri*)
1 green chilli, chopped (*hari mirch*)
2-3 tbsp chopped fresh coriander (*dhania patta*)
Salt to taste (*namak*)
3-4 tbsp sweet tamarind chutney (*imli ki chutney*), ref Contents
2-3 tbsp green chutney (*hara chutney*), ref Contents

53

METHOD
1. In a *kadhai*, dry roast the puffed rice for 2-3 minutes on low heat till crisp. Remove and cool.
2. In another bowl, mix together the salt, potatoes, cucumber and green chillies with the chutneys.
3. Mix in the puffed rice gently.
4. Garnish with chopped fresh coriander and serve.

NOTE
✓ Tomatoes and raw mango can be further additions.

KOSAMBARI
Split Legume Salad

Cooking food uncovered where possible, allows excess Vata to escape into the atmosphere. This is useful when cooking lentils and legumes or other Vata-dominated foods. When using a pressure cooker, allow the steam to escape for a minute or two before putting on the whistle.

INGREDIENTS
For the Salad
2 cups grated carrots (*gajar*)
1 cup grated fresh coconut (*nariyal*)
2 tbsp chopped fresh coriander (*dhania patta*)
1 tsp lemon juice (*limbu*)

For the Seasoning
¼ tsp mustard seeds (*rai*)
1 green chilli, deseeded & chopped (*hari mirch*)
A pinch of asafoetida (*hing*)
3-4 curry leaves (*kari patta*)
2 tsp oil (*tel*)

54

METHOD
1. Mix together all the ingredients for the salad.
2. Heat oil for the seasoning and add the mustard seeds. Once they crackle, add the asafoetida, green chillies and curry leaves. Mix into the salad.
3. Garnish with chopped fresh coriander and serve.

NOTES
✓ Similar *koshambari* can be made with split yellow *moong dal* (soak the *moong dal* for 1-2 hours before you need to make the salad). It can be added to the carrot along with the chopped cucumber.

KABULI CHANA SUNDAL
Chickpea Salad with Spices

Vegetables of the 'nightshade' family (potatoes, tomatoes, capsicum, green chilli peppers, brinjals), are recommended for limited use by Ayurveda because of their pungent and sour post-digestive effect. Cumin, turmeric and mustard seeds are said to contain adverse effects, and are not recommended as staple items in the diet. Modern science recognizes that these vegetables contain alkaloid toxins (particularly their leaves), which have adverse effects on the human system. Try to replace potatoes with sweet potatoes and yams where possible. Sundal *is made from different varieties of beans during* Navratri *in southern India.*

INGREDIENTS

1 cup chickpeas (*kabuli chana*)
¼ tsp mustard seeds (*rai*)
¼ tsp black beans (*urad dal*)
¼ tsp Bengal gram (*chana dal*)
1 green chilli, finely chopped (*hari mirch*)
OR 1-2 dried, whole red chillies (*Kashmiri mirch*)
1tsp finely chopped fresh ginger (*adrak*)
6-8 curry leaves (*kari patta*)
A pinch of asafoetida (*hing*)
1 tbsp fresh grated coconut (*nariyal*)
1-2 tbsp finely chopped raw mango (can be substituted with *amchur* powder)
1 tbsp oil (*tel*)

METHOD

1. Soak the chickpeas overnight. Next morning, cook them in a pressure cooker with some salt, till tender. Drain and cool.
2. In a frying pan/*kadhai*, heat the oil and add the mustard seeds. Once the seeds pop, put in the asafoetida, *chana* and *urad dal*s, followed by the green chillies, ginger and curry leaves. Add the *kabuli chana* and mix well. Adjust the salt if needed. Finally add the raw mango. Garnish with the coconut and serve.

VEGETABLES & LENTILS

Annapurna Devi: It is said that Lord Shiva once lost all his belongings to Devi Parvati in a game of dice. Miffed at the loss, he went off to roam the forests, where he met Lord Vishnu, who persuaded him to return and play again to win back his possessions. The ease of his subsequent win aroused the suspicions of the Goddess and Lord Vishnu revealed himself, stating that he had determined the course of the game even though both players were under the illusion that they were playing under regular conditions.

The concept of 'illusion' was then discussed at length and ultimately Lord Shiva opined that everything in the world, including the food we eat, is illusory. This statement angered the Goddess, who disappeared, saying that if food was an illusion, then so was she! The disappearance of the Devi disrupted the seasons, causing drought, famine and widespread hardship to all creatures in the cosmos. Lord Shiva realized that he was incomplete without his Shakti and prayed for the restoration of the natural order. It is then that Goddess Parvati appeared in the city of Kashi and brought the world the blessing of food. Hence, she is also worshipped as Annapurna Devi.

- Lauki ki Sabzi
- Beans Kari
- Avial
- Keerai Sundal
- Palak Paneer
- Mooli ki Bhujji
- Moong-Palak Dal
- Chana-Lauki Dal
- Urad Dal Amtee
- Panchmel Dal
- Sambhar

LAUKI KI SABZI
Bottle Gourd

The three doshas *move in a cycle through the day and night, each dominating specific time periods.* Kapha *predominates from about 6 am to 10 am, followed by* Pitta *from 10 am to 2 pm, and then by* Vata *from 2 pm to 6 pm; and again in the same order through the evening and night. When the body is in balance,* Kapha *moistens, lubricates and strengthens the system in its time;* Pitta *digests and transforms the food during its slot; and* Vata *causes the movement of energy and communication between different systems during the period of its domination. The human life cycle also moves through periods of* Kapha *domination (growth during childhood); then* Pitta *(vigorous energy, fiery ambition and action); followed by the* Vata *period when we grow older.*

INGREDIENTS

500 gms bottle gourd (*lauki*)

¼ tsp cumin seeds (*jeera*)

¼ tsp turmeric powder (*haldi*)

A pinch of asafoetida (*hing*)

1tsp finely chopped ginger (*adrak*)

Salt to taste (*namak*)

1-2 tsp lemon juice (*limbu*)

2 tsp clarified butter (*ghee*)

METHOD

1. Peel the bottle gourd and chop into 1" pieces.
2. Heat the *ghee* in a pressure cooker and add the cumin seeds. Once they splutter, add the turmeric powder, asafoetida and ginger. Give a quick stir before adding the bottle gourd. Mix well and add 2-3 tbsp water and salt. Pressure cook for one whistle, then reduce heat to allow it to simmer for 5 minutes.
3. Remove from heat and allow the steam to escape. Check if done.
4. Add lemon juice and adjust seasoning if required.
5. Serve hot with *rotis* or *parathas*.

58

BEANS KARI
Stir Fried Beans

Properties of common spices ~
  Sattvik – *Cardamom, Coriander, Fennel, Cumin, Fenugreek & Saffron*
  Rajasic – *Asafoetida, Black Pepper, Cinnamon, Cloves, Ginger, Mint & Ajwain*
  Tamasic – *Garlic & Onion*

INGREDIENTS

3 cups finely chopped French beans (*fansi*)
2-3 tbsp freshly grated coconut (*nariyal*)
4-5 curry leaves (*kari patta*)
¼ tsp mustard seeds (*rai*)
½ tsp black beans, split & dehusked (*urad dal*)
1 whole red chilli (*lal mirch*)
1-2 tsp oil (*tel*)
1 cup water
Salt to taste (*namak*)

59

METHOD

1. Boil the water with a pinch of salt. Add the beans and cook over medium heat till they become tender (the water should be almost absorbed). Drain and set aside.
2. In a frying pan/*kadhai*, heat the oil and add the mustard seeds. Once they splutter, add the *urad dal* and curry leaves. Stir till lightly browned. Add the red chilli.
3. Add the chopped beans and stir for a minute before removing from heat.
4. Adjust the seasoning before adding the grated coconut. Mix well and serve hot.

Sattvik Spices

Rajasic Spices

Tamasic Spices

AVIAL
Mixed Vegetables in Coconut Gravy

INGREDIENTS

¼ cup ash gourd, peeled (*turi*)

1 drumstick, chopped into 3" pieces (*munga /sengue*)

¼ cup peeled & chopped carrots (*gajar*)

¼ cup chopped pumpkin (*bhopla*)

¼ cup chopped beans (*fansi*)

6-8 curry leaves (*kari patta*)

1 cup freshly grated coconut (*nariyal*)

1-2 green chillies (*hari mirch*)

3-4 tbsp curd, whisked smooth (*dahi*)

METHOD

1. Boil water with turmeric and salt and add the vegetables, beginning with the ones that take the longest to cook and ending with those that cook fast. Cook till just tender. Drain and set aside. Save the water in which the vegetables have been cooked.
2. Grind the coconut and green chillies into a paste and set aside.
3. Heat a frying pan/*kadhai* on medium heat and put in the coconut paste, curd, curry leaves and mixed vegetables. Add the reserved water and simmer till a thick sauce has formed. Adjust the seasoning and remove from heat.
4. Add the coconut oil and fresh curry leaves.
5. Serve hot with rice

NOTES

✓ Any vegetables that hold their shape when cooked, can be used for this curry.

✓ If you are not used to the taste of coconut oil as a garnish, skip that step.

KEERAI SUNDAL
Stir Fried Greens

Ahartatttva *or the science of dietetics as laid down in the* Charaka Samhita, *examines the effects of foods on humans from the perspective of the resulting changes in physiology and temperament, as well as cooking method used and the season. In fact, seasonality was a vital factor in choosing foods for medication or daily use. But with most fruits, vegetables and herbs being constantly transported across the world these days, the advantages of consuming local and seasonal produce has been nullified.*

INGREDIENTS

2 bundles spinach or other greens, washed & chopped (*palak/saag*)
¼ tsp mustard seeds (*rai*)
¼ tsp black beans, split & dehusked (*urad dal*)
¼ tsp turmeric powder (*haldi*)
A pinch of asafoetida (*hing*)
1 tbsp freshly grated coconut (*nariyal*)
Salt to taste (*namak*)
1 whole red chilli (*lal mirch*)
1-2 tsp oil (*tel*)

62

METHOD
1. Wash the greens thoroughly, drain and chop roughly. Put into a pan with salt and turmeric and allow to wilt. Cook till the water has been absorbed.
2. In a frying pan, heat the oil and add the mustard seeds. Once they splutter, add the *urad dal*, asafoetida and red chilli.
3. Add the spinach and mix well.
4. Garnish with grated coconut and serve hot.

NOTE
✓ A tsp of *sambhar* powder can be added to the greens to give more flavour.

PALAK PANEER
Indian Cottage Cheese in Spinach Gravy

What is **Shat-Rasa-Vidya?** *Ayurveda has designed the* Shat-Rasa Vidya *or Science of Six Tastes. These six tastes are:* Lavana *(Salty),* Amla *(Sour),* Katu *(Pungent),* Tikta *(Bitter),* Madhur *(Sweet) and* Kashaya *(Astringent). In Ayurveda, there are also Five Elements, known as* Pancha-mahabhutas, *meaning 'five great elemental forces', which are* Akasha *(Ether),* Vayu *(Air),* Agni *(Fire),* Jala *(Water), and* Prthvi *(Earth). Each of these is important, in relation to both the* doshas *(humors) and* rasas *(tastes). For example,* Kapha-dosha *(Water or a combination of Earth and Water);* Pitta-dosha *(Fire or a combination of Fire and Water); and the* Vata-dosha *(Wind or a combination of Air and Ether). Likewise, the Six Tastes are linked to the Elemental Forces* (Pancha-mahabhutas) *and the Humors* (Doshas).

Rasa (Taste)	*Dosha (Humor)*	*Bhuta (Element)*
Lavana *(salty)*	Kapha + Pitta	*Water and Fire*
Amla *(sour)*	Pitta + Kapha	*Earth and Fire*
Katu *(pungent)*	Vata + Pitta	*Fire and Air*
Tikta *(bitter)*	Vata	*Air and Ether*
Madhur *(sweet)*	Kapha	*Earth and Water*
Kashaya *(astringent)*	Vata	*Air and Earth*

INGREDIENTS
2 bunches spinach (*palak*)
1 cup cottage cheese, cut into 1" pieces (*paneer*)
2" piece fresh ginger, washed & peeled (*adrak*)
1-2 green chillies (*hari mirch*)
¼ tsp cumin seeds (*jeera*)
A pinch of turmeric powder (*haldi*)
2 tsp clarified butter (*ghee*)

METHOD

1. Wash the spinach thoroughly. Boil a cup of water in a pan with a pinch of salt and add the spinach. Blanch for 2 minutes. Drain and plunge into cold water to preserve the colour. Cool.
2. Soak the *paneer* cubes in warm water till required.
3. Pulse the spinach, ginger and green chillies in a blender till a coarse purée has formed.
4. Heat the *ghee* in a frying pan/*kadhai* and add the cumin seeds. Once they crackle, put in the turmeric powder and stir.
5. Add the spinach purée and mix well. Allow to simmer for 5 minutes.
6. Drain the *paneer* cubes and mix into the gravy.
7. Warm through and serve.

64

Shat-Rasa: Science Of Six Tastes

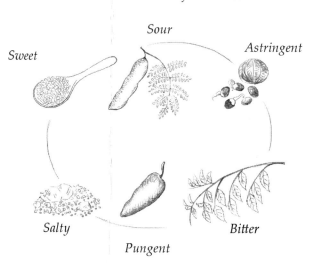

MOOLI KI BHUJJI
Stir Fried Radish Greens

Moong *or* Masha, *as it was called in the Vedic period, is the most nourishing and easily digested of all lentils, according to Ayurveda. It has the ability to balance all three* doshas *and detoxify the system while setting it right.*

INGREDIENTS

6-8 medium-sized white radishes with leaves (*mooli*)
Salt to taste (*namak*)
¼ tsp carom seeds (*ajwain*)
1 whole red chilli (*lal mirch*)
A pinch of asafoetida (*hing*)
A pinch of dried mango powder (*amchur*)
1 tbsp oil, preferably mustard oil (*rai ka tel*)

65

METHOD

1. Remove the radish leaves and wash well in running water. Discard any leaves that have turned yellow or are damaged. Drain and chop finely.
2. Peel 2-3 radishes and chop into small pieces (keep the rest to use in *parathas/ baingan-mooli* etc).
3. In a pressure cooker, steam the chopped leaves and radishes with a pinch of salt (1-2 whistles). When cool, remove and squeeze out the excess water. Set aside.
4. In a *kadhai*, heat the oil and add the *ajwain*. Once it splutters, add the asafoetida and red chilli. Give a quick stir and add the steamed radish and leaves. Stir to mix the spices and vegetable and cook on medium heat for about 4-5 minutes.
5. Adjust the salt and add the *amchur* powder. Mix well and serve hot.

NOTE

✓ Radish enhances the digestion and is thus served grated with ginger, lemon juice and salt, as an accompaniment to meals

MOONG-PALAK DAL
Split Mung Beans with Spinach

All dals (except moong*), produce gas and the* tarka *or* chhaunk (ghee *flavoured with spices), is what nullifies this while making the dal easier to digest. It is important to include the* tarka *in all lentil preparations.*

INGREDIENTS

1 cup mung beans (*moong dal*)
1 bunch spinach leaves (*palak*)
2 medium-sized tomatoes, chopped (*tamatar*)
1 green chilli, chopped (*hari mirch*)
2 tbsp finely chopped fresh ginger (*adrak*)
A pinch of asafoetida (*hing*)
¼ tsp cumin seeds (*jeera*)
¼ tsp turmeric powder (*haldi*)
Salt to taste (*namak*)
1 tbsp clarified butter (*ghee*)
1 tbsp lemon juice (*limbu*)

METHOD

1. Soak the *moong dal* for 20-30 minutes.
2. Wash the spinach leaves thoroughly, drain and remove the stalks. Chop the leaves fine.
3. Heat the *ghee* in the pressure cooker and add the cumin seeds. Once they splutter, add the asafoetida, turmeric powder, green chillies and half the ginger. Fry for a minute. Add the tomatoes and cook till done.
4. Add the *moong dal* and chopped spinach and mix well. Add 3½ cups water and pressure cook for one whistle. Remove from heat and allow the steam to escape.
5. Garnish with chopped coriander and ginger and serve hot.

CHANA-LAUKI DAL
Split Bengal Gram with Bottle Gourd

Soaking foodgrains, legumes and lentils before cooking is important because it reduces the vata *present in them and the increased moisture helps the digestion of the cooked food by the digestive fire.*

INGREDIENTS

1 cup Bengal gram (*chana dal*)
2½ cups bottle gourd, chopped into ½ inch pieces (*doodhi/ lauki*)
2 medium-sized tomatoes, chopped (*tamatar*)
1-2 green chillies, chopped (*hari mirch*)
1½ tbsp finely grated/chopped fresh ginger (*hari mirch*)
A pinch of asafoetida (*hing*)
¼ tsp cumin seeds (*jeera*)
¼ tsp turmeric powder (*haldi*)
Salt to taste (*namak*)
1 tbsp clarified butter (*ghee*)
2-3 tsp lemon juice (*limbu*)
1-2 tbsp finely chopped fresh coriander (*dhania patta*)
2 cups water

METHOD
1. Soak the *chana dal* 6-8 hours before using.
2. Heat the *ghee* in a pressure cooker and add the cumin seeds. Once they splutter, add the asafoetida, followed by the green chillies, ginger and turmeric. Stir-fry for a minute on medium heat. Add the tomatoes and cook for 3-5 minutes till soft.
3. Add the chopped gourd and *dal*. Mix well for a minute. Add the water and salt and pressure cook for 1 whistle. Reduce heat and cook for 10-15 minutes.
4. Take off the heat and allow the steam to escape. Check to see if the *dal* is done.
5. Remove into a serving bowl, add 1-2 tsp of lemon juice and mix well. Garnish with fresh coriander before serving.

URAD DAL AMTEE
Spicy Split Black Gram

Life remains unharmed when one eats with restraint, refraining from foods that have proven disagreeable. ~ Thirukural

INGREDIENTS

For the *Kala Masala*

1 cup coriander seeds (*dhanadal*)

¼ cup cumin seeds (*jeera*)

1/3 cup white sesame seeds (*til*)

2 tbsp cloves (*laung*)

2 tbsp black cardamom seeds (*elaichi*)

1" piece cinnamon (*dalchini*)

2 tbsp black peppercorns (*sabut kala mirch*)

2-3 bay leaves (*tej patta*)

1-2 tsp oil (*tel*)

For the *Dal*

3 tbsp pigeon peas (*tur dal*)

3 tbsp black beans with skin (*chilka urad dal*)

2 tbsp grated fresh coconut (*nariyal*)

1 tbsp finely chopped ginger (*adrak*)

1 finely chopped green chilli (*hari mirch*)

¼ tsp *kala masala* (also known as *goda masala*)

1 tbsp tamarind pulp (*imli*) /6-8 *Garciana Indica* pieces (*kokum*)/ 2 tsp lemon juice (*limbu*)

3-4 curry leaves (*kari patta*)

A pinch of asafoetida (*hing*)

¼ tsp mustard seeds (*rai*)

Salt to taste (*namak*)

1 tbsp clarified butter (*ghee*)

METHOD

For the *Kala Masala*

1. Heat oil in a frying pan and roast all the masala ingredients, stirring constantly till they turn brown.
2. Remove from heat and allow to cool before grinding to a powder. This *masala* should be dark brown.

For the *Dal*

1. Soak the *dal*s separately for 15-30 minutes.
2. Add the ginger and green chillies to the combined *dal*s and pressure cook with 2 cups water, till done. Remove from heat.
3. Add the turmeric, salt, and grated coconut, followed by the souring agent you have chosen.
4. For the *tadka*, heat the *ghee* in a ladle or small saucepan. Add the mustard seeds and after they splutter, add in the asafoetida and curry leaves. Pour onto the *dal*.
5. Serve hot with rice.

69

NOTES

✓ This *dal* should be of medium consistency. In case it requires more water, add boiled water and simmer before adding the coconut etc.
✓ *Dagadphool* (a kind of lichen, also called black stone flower), is also added to the *kala masala* – if it is not easily available, skip it.
✓ *Garam masala* can be used as a substitute for *kala masala*.

PANCHMEL DAL
Mixed Lentils

INGREDIENTS

1/5 cup pigeon peas (*tur dal*)
1/5 cup mung beans (*moong dal*)
1/5 cup red lentils (*masoor dal*)
1/5 cup black beans (*urad dal*)
1/5 cup Bengal gram (*chana dal*)
¼ tsp asafoetida (*hing*)
½ tsp black pepper powder (*kala mirch*)
¼ tsp *garam masala*
½ tsp coriander powder (*dhania* powder)
2 medium-sized tomatoes, chopped (*tamatar*)
1-2 green chillies, chopped fine (*hari mirch*)
2-3 tbsp finelt chopped fresh ginger (*adrak*)
1 medium-sized onion, chopped fine (*pyaaz*)
1 tsp grated garlic (*lasun*)
Salt to taste (*namak*)
2 whole red chillies (*lal mirch*)
½ tsp cumin seeds (*jeera*)
1-2 tbsp clarified butter (*ghee*)
1" piece cinnamon (*dalchini*)
2-3 cloves (*laung*)
2 tbsp chopped, fresh coriander (*dhania patta*)
2 cups water

70

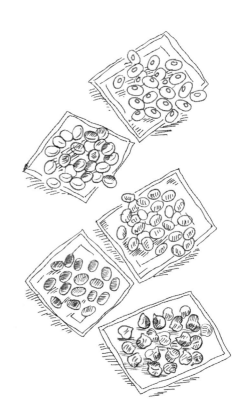

METHOD

1. Soak all the *dals* for 15-30 minutes and pressure-cook with 2 cups of water, salt and turmeric. Also put in the ginger and green chillies. Remove from heat and once the steam has escaped, check if the *dals* are tender.
2. In a frying pan/*kadhai*, heat the *ghee*. Add the cumin seeds and once they begin to crackle, put in the asafoetida, whole red chillies, cloves and cinnamon. Stir.
3. Add the garlic and onions and sauté till the onions are translucent. Add the tomatoes and fry till they are cooked and soft.
4. Put in the pepper powder, coriander powder and *garam masala*. Adjust salt if needed and simmer for 3-5 minutes. Garnish with fresh coriander and serve hot.

NOTE

✓ This is a relatively simple version of *dal* and can also have chickpeas, *rajma* or dried white peas added to it.

71

SAMBHAR
Yellow Lentils with Tamarind & Vegetables

INGREDIENTS

For the *Sambhar* Powder

2 cups coriander seeds (*dhanadal*)
8-10 red chillies or to taste (*lal mirch*)
5 tsp cumin seeds (*jeera*)
2 tsp fenugreek seeds (*methi dana*)
1/8 tsp oil (*tel*)

For the *Sambhar*

½ cup pigeon peas (*tur dal*)
2 tbsp tamarind pulp, thick (*imli*)
¼ tsp turmeric powder (*haldi*)
2 cups, chopped into 1" pieces: ladyfinger/ eggplant/ radish (*bhindi/baigan/mooli*))

10-12 baby/ pearl onions (*pyaaz*)
¼ tsp mustard seeds (*rai*)
A pinch of asafoetida (*hing*)
¼ tsp black beans (*urad dal*)
Salt to taste (*namak*)
6-8 curry leaves (*kari patta*)
1-2 tsp *sambhar* powder
1 tbsp oil (*tel*)

METHOD

For the *Masala*

1. In a flat-bottomed pan, dry roast each of the ingredients (except the red chillies) separately and remove from heat.
2. For the red chillies, add a few drops of oil and roast on gentle heat till they start changing colour. Cool and dry-grind into a powder.

For the *Sambhar*

1. Pressure cook the *tur dal* with 2 cups of water after adding a little salt and turmeric powder. Remove from heat. When cool, blend with a whisk.
2. In a *kadhai*, heat the oil and add the mustard seeds. Once they splutter, add the *urad dal*, asafoetida and curry leaves, followed by the onions. Add the chopped vegetables and stir-fry for a few minutes.
3. Put in 1 cup of water. Cook covered on medium heat till the vegetables are done.
4. Add the tamarind paste and *sambhar* powder and mix well, ensuring that there are no lumps. Add the pressure-cooked *dal* and serve hot.

NOTES

✓ Every household in south India has its own recipe for *sambhar* powder. Depending on taste, you can add *urad dal*, grated coconut, dried curry leaves etc.
✓ If using drumsticks, cut into 2-3" pieces, parboil in salted water, then add.

RICE

Rice is one of the most widespread foods around the world. According to Ayurveda, it has cooling properties and is easy to digest, particularly when aged for 1-2 years. The greatest nutritive value is obtained when rice is hand-pounded and unpolished. The outer layers are believed to be beneficial in maintaining healthy skin. One can combine rice with husked lentils, nuts and herbs, to compensate for the loss of nutrients from polishing rice.

Annaprashana, *also known as* annaprashana vidhi, annaprasan, *or* anna-prasanam, *is a Hindu rite-of-passage ritual that marks an infant's first intake of food other than milk. The term* annaprashana *literally means 'eating of food'. The ceremony is usually arranged in consultation with a priest on an auspicious date. Commonly referred to in English as First Rice, the ceremony is usually done when the child is about 6 months old (some Hindu communities do it later). It is an occasion for celebration with the extended family, friends and neighbours. The mother or grandmother will prepare a small bowl of* payesh *(boiled rice, milk & sugar), which is blessed in a brief* puja. *Usually a senior male family member (grandfather or uncle), then feeds the child a small spoonful of the payesh. Other members of the family then take turns to give the child a taste. The feeding ceremony is often followed with a game, in which the child is presented with a tray containing a number of objects (including a bangle or jewel (symbolising wealth), a book (symbolising learning), a pen (symbolising career, and a clay pot with earth/soil (symbolising property). The child's future direction and prospects in life are indicated by the object which the child prefers to hold and play with.*

- Limbu Bhaat
- Vaangi Bhaat (Brinjal Rice)
- Puliyodharai Bhaat
- Thayir Sadam
- Tehri

- Ven Pongal
- Moong Dal Khichdi
- Tur/Arhar Dal Khichdi
- Bisi Bele Huliyana

LIMBU BHAAT
Lemon Rice

INGREDIENTS

2 cups rice
2 tbsp lemon juice (*limbu*)
¼ tsp mustard seeds (*rai*)
A pinch of asafoetida (*hing*)
¼ tsp turmeric powder (*haldi*)
2 green chillies, chopped fine (*hari mirch*)
6-8 curry leaves (*kari patta*)
1-2 tsp oil (*tel*)
10-15 *chana dal*, split & dehusked
A few drops clarified butter (*ghee*)
Salt to taste (*namak*)

METHOD

1. Cook rice in water, adding a few drops of *ghee*. The grains of rice should be separate and not over done. Set aside to cool.
2. In a frying pan, heat the oil and add the mustard seeds. Once they splutter, put in the *chana dal* and brown gently.
3. Add the turmeric powder and asafoetida, followed by the green chillies and curry leaves. Stir for a few seconds. Remove from heat.
4. Add salt and lemon juice.
5. Mix the cooked rice into this and warm through. Serve hot.

NOTES

✓ For this purpose, rice is best cooked in an open pan (to drain off the excess water once rice is done) or rice cooker.
✓ Finely chopped coriander can also be added to the rice as a garnish.

VAANGI BHAAT
Brinjal Rice

INGREDIENTS
For the *Vaangi Bhaat Masala*
2 tsp oil (*tel*)
1 tbsp coriander seeds (*dhanadal*)
1" piece cinnamon (*dalchini*)
2-3 cloves (*laung*)
2-3 dried red chillies, whole (*Kashmiri mirch*)
3 tsp Bengal Gram (*chana dal*)
2 tsp Black gram, split & dehusked (*urad dal*)
1 tbsp grated coconut (*nariyal*)

For the Rice
2 cups rice (*chawal*)
1-2 tbsp tamarind purée (*imli*)
2-3 cups chopped brinjals, into 1" pieces (*baigan*)
¼ tsp turmeric powder (*haldi*)
2 tbsp *vangi bhat masala*
Salt to taste (*namak*)
¼ tsp mustard seeds (*rai*)
6-8 curry leaves (*kari patta*)
2 green chillies, finely chopped (*hari mirch*)
A few drops clarified butter (*ghee*)

75

METHOD

1. Heat oil in a pan and add the ingredients for the *masala*. Roast on gentle heat till they release an aroma. Remove from heat and set aside to cool. Then grind to a fine powder.
2. Cook rice in water, adding a few drops of *ghee*. The grains of rice should be separate and not over-done. Set aside to cool.
3. In a frying pan, heat the oil and add the mustard seeds. Once they splutter, put in the green chillies and curry leaves, stirring for about 5 seconds.
4. Add the turmeric powder and the chopped brinjals. Cover and cook on medium heat till done.
5. Add the *vangi bhat masala* and tamarind purée and salt to taste.
6. Mix in the cooked rice and warm though. Serve hot.

NOTE

✓ A few cashewnuts, fried in *ghee*, can be added as a garnish to the rice.

PULIYODHARAI BHAAT
Tamarind Rice
This rice is often served as temple prasad.

INGREDIENTS
2 cups rice (*chawal*)
¼ tsp turmeric powder (*haldi*)
A pinch of asafoetida (*hing*)
½ cup tamarind purée (*imli*)
½ cup roasted peanuts, skinned (*mungfalli*)
½ cup sesame oil (*til ka tel*)
Salt to taste (*namak*)
2 dried red chillies, whole (*Kashmiri mirch*)
¼ tsp mustard seeds (*rai*)
½ cup Bengal gram (*chana dal*)
10-15 curry leaves (*kari patta*)
A few drops of clarified butter (*ghee*)

METHOD
1. Cook the rice in water, adding a few drops of *ghee*. The grains of rice should be separate and not over-done. Set aside to cool.
2. In a frying pan, heat 1 tablespoon of oil and add the mustard seeds. Once they splutter, put in the *chana dal* and curry leaves.
3. Add the red chillies and fry till they turn bright red. Then add the peanuts and asafoetida. Sauté for 15 secs. Add the tamarind purée, turmeric powder and salt.
4. Cover and cook on gentle heat till a thick sauce has formed.
5. Add the remaining oil and mix well.
6. Mix in the cooked rice with a gentle hand and let it rest for 10 minutes so that the rice absorbs all the flavours. Serve warm.

THAYIR SADAM
Curd Rice

INGREDIENTS

1½ cups rice (*chawal*)
2½ cups yoghurt (*dahi*)
¾ cup milk (*dudh*)
6-8 curry leaves (*kari patta*)
1 tbsp chopped fresh coriander (*dhania patta*)
¼ tsp mustard seeds (*rai*)
A pinch of asafoetida (*hing*)
1-2 green chillies, chopped fine (*hari mirch*)
1" piece ginger, peeled & chopped fine (*adrak*)
Salt to taste (*namak*)
1 tsp oil (*tel*)

METHOD
1. Cook the rice till almost mushy. Mash with the ladle and mix in the milk. There should be no lumps. Set aside.
2. Mix in the yoghurt and salt.
3. In a frying pan, heat the oil and put in the mustard seeds. Once the seeds splutter, add the asafoetida, green chillies, and ginger. Stir-fry for a few seconds.
4. Add to the rice and mix well.
5. Serve warm or cold as preferred.

NOTES
✓ Curd rice is traditionally the last course in any south Indian meal, but does well as a light but filling meal during the hot summer months as well.
✓ Finely chopped cucumber and/or grated carrot, can also be added to this dish.

TEHRI
Rice with Cauliflower, Potato & Peas

INGREDIENTS

1 cup rice, preferably Basmati (*chawal*)
1 medium-sized potato, cut into 1" cubes (*alu*)
1 cup 1"long cauliflower florets (*phool gobhi*)
½ cup green peas (*matar*)
2 black cardamoms (*elaichi*)
¼ tsp cumin seeds (*jeera*)
¼ tsp turmeric powder (*haldi*)
Salt to taste (*namak*)
1 green chilli, chopped fine (*hari mirch*)
1½ tbsp thinly sliced fresh ginger (*adrak*)
1-2 tbsp clarified butter (*ghee*)

79

METHOD

1. Wash the rice and soak for 10-15 minutes.
2. Heat the *ghee* in a pan and add the cumin seeds. Once they splutter, add the cardamom pods, sliced ginger, green chilli and turmeric powder. Give a quick stir before adding the cauliflower florets, potato cubes and peas. Mix well. Cook on medium heat for 2-3 minutes before mixing in the rice gently.
3. Add 2½ cups water and bring to a boil. Reduce the heat to bring the water to a simmer, then cover and cook for 15 minutes. Stir gently once or twice as it cooks to ensure the rice does not stick to the bottom of the pan.
4. Turn off the heat, leave to rest for another 10 minutes.
5. Serve hot with yoghurt.

NOTE

✓ Fresh green chutney goes well as an accompaniment with this dish as well.

VEN PONGAL
Rice & Yellow Mung Beans Porridge with Black Peppercorns & Curry Leaves

INGREDIENTS

1 cup rice (*chawal*)
½ cup mung beansplit & dehusked (*moong dal*)
8-10 cashewnuts (*kaju*)
2 whole, dried red chillies (*Kashmiri mirch*)
¼ tsp asafoetida (*hing*)
10-12 peppercorns (*kala mirch*)
8-10 curry leaves (*kari patta*)
Salt to taste (*namak*)
2 tbsp clarified butter (*ghee*)

80

METHOD

1. In a frying pan, heat half the *ghee* and add the *moong dal*. Gently roast on low heat till it emits an aroma and is tinged pink. Take off the heat and keep aside.
2. Cook the *dal* and rice with salt in a pressure cooker (with 3½ cups of water), for 3 whistles. Remove from heat and let the steam escape.
3. In the frying pan, heat the remaining *ghee* and add the cashewnuts and fry till they turn light pink. Remove and set aside.
4. Add the red chillies and fry till they turn bright red before putting in the asafoetida, peppercorns and curry leaves.
5. Add the tempering to the cooked *dal*-rice mixture.
6. Serve hot with coconut chutney and *sambhar* (see Contents, *Vegetables & Lentils*).

NOTE

✓ Cumin seeds, grated ginger and chopped green chillies can be added to the seasoning.

MOONG DAL KHICHDI
Rice & Split Green Mung Beans Porridge

INGREDIENTS

1 cup rice
¾ cup mung beans, split & dehusked (*chilka moong dal*)
1 tbsp clarified butter (*ghee*)
A pinch of asafoetida (*hing*)
Salt to taste (*namak*)
¼ tsp turmeric powder (*haldi*)
¼ tsp coriander seeds (*dhanadal*)
1 green chilli, finely chopped (*hari mirch*)
1 tbsp finely chopped fresh ginger (*adrak*)
6-7 cups water

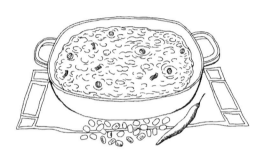

81

METHOD
1. Wash the rice and *dal* well. Soak for half an hour together.
2. In a pressure cooker, heat the *ghee* and add the cumin seeds. Once they splutter, add the turmeric, green chillies and ginger. Stir for a few seconds and add the rice and *dal*. Mix well.
3. Add the salt and water and cook for 3 whistles. Remove from heat and let the steam escape.
4. Serve hot with yoghurt and pickle.

NOTES
✓ This *khichdi* can also be made with whole *moong dal* without the husk removed.
✓ The rice and *dal* should be well cooked and mushy.

TUR/ARHAR DAL KHICHDI
Rice & Pigeon Peas Porridge
Purayed asanenardham trtiyam udakena tu vayoh sancaranartham tu caturtham avasesayet
(One should fill the stomach half with food, one quarter with water, and the
one quarter remaining for the movement of air) ~ *Bhagavad Gita*

INGREDIENTS

¾ cup pigeon peas (*tur dal*)

1 cup rice (*chawal*)

¼ tsp cumin seeds (*jeera*)

¼ tsp turmeric powder (*haldi*)

A large pinch of asafoetida (*hing*)

1-2 green chillies, chopped fine (*hari mirch*)

2 tbsp finely chopped fresh ginger (*adrak*)

1 tbsp clarified butter (*ghee*)

4 cups water

82

METHOD

1. Wash the rice and *dal* well. Soak together for about half an hour.
2. Heat half the *ghee* in a pressure cooker and add the cumin seeds. Once they splutter, add the green chillies and ginger, followed by the asafoetida and turmeric. Give it a quick stir.
3. Add the rice, *dal* and salt to taste before putting in 4 cups of water.
4. Pressure cook for 2whistles. Take off the heat and let the steam escape.
5. Add the remaining *ghee* and mix well before serving hot.

NOTES

✓ The grains of rice and *dal* should be separate and not mashed together.
✓ Accompaniments can include fresh green chutney, yoghurt and papad.

BISI BELE HULIYANA
Rice, Pigeon Peas, Vegetables & Tamarind Porridge

INGREDIENTS
For the *Huliyana Masala*
2 tbsp Bengal gram (*chana dal)*
1 tbsp black beans, split &dehusked (*urad dal)*
2 green cardamoms (*hari elaichi*)
2 cloves (*laung*)
1" piece cinnamon (*dalchini*)
15-20 fenugreek seeds (*methi dana*)
2 whole, dried red chillies (*Kashmiri mirch*)
2 tbsp desiccated coconut (*nariyal*)

For the *Bisi Bele Huilyana*
1 cup rice (*chawal*)
2/3 cup pigeon peas (*tur dal*)
1/3 cup chopped carrot (*gajar*)
1/3 cup chopped French beans (*fansi*)
¼ cup small-cubed potato (*alu*)
¼ cup chopped onion (*pyaaz*)
6-8 curry leaves (*kari patta*)
2 tbsp tamarind paste (*imli*)
1 tsp mustard seeds (*rai*)
A pinch of asafoetida (*hing*)
1 tbsp clarified butter (*ghee*)
Salt to taste (*namak*)
1" piece jaggery (*gur*)

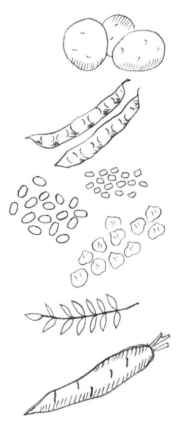

METHOD

For the *Masala*

1. Dry roast all the ingredients for the *masala* (except the coconut), on medium heat. Set aside to cool.
2. Grind all the cooled ingredients with the desiccated coconut, to a fine powder.

For the *Bisi Bele Bhath*

1. Soak the *tur dal* for half an hour.
2. Pressure cook the *dal* with some turmeric and salt till soft. Remove from the cooker and set aside.
3. In a pressure cooker, heat the *ghee* and add the mustard seeds. Once they pop, add the turmeric, asafoetida and curry leaves, followed by the chopped vegetables. Add half the *huliyana masala* and mix well. Stir-fry for 2-3 minutes before adding the rice and cooked *dal*.
4. Add the jaggery, 3-4 cups of water and salt to taste and pressure cook for 2-3 whistles. Take the cooker off the heat, allow the pressure to fall and check if the *dal* and rice are done.
5. Mix the remaining *huliyana masala* and tamarind paste and add this to the cooked *dal* and rice. Adjust salt if required.
6. Serve hot.

NOTE

✓ The mixture can be tempered again with some more mustard seeds, curry leaves and dried red chillies and also garnished with fried cashewnuts.

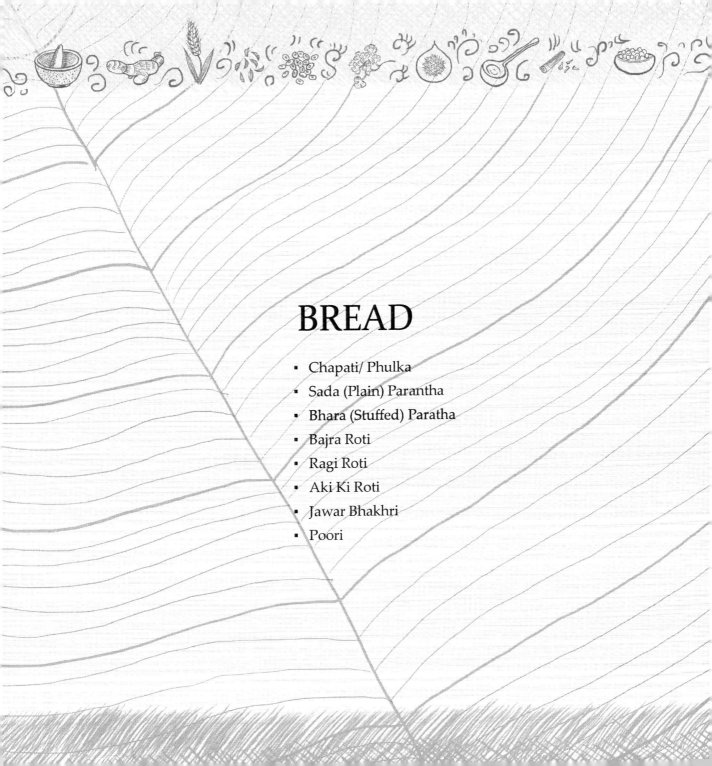

BREAD

- Chapati/ Phulka
- Sada (Plain) Parantha
- Bhara (Stuffed) Paratha
- Bajra Roti
- Ragi Roti
- Aki Ki Roti
- Jawar Bhakhri
- Poori

CHAPATI / PHULKA
Plain Puffed Indian Bread

INGREDIENTS

2¼ cups whole wheat flour (*atta*)

1 cup water

2-3 tsp clarified butter, optional (*ghee*)

METHOD

1. Set aside ¼ cup of the flour for use while rolling the *chapatis*.
2. Put the remaining flour into a mixing bowl or *paraat*. Adding a little water at a time, knead into a smooth dough. The dough is ready when it pulls away from the sides of the bowl. Cover with moist cloth and allow to rest for 30 minutes.
3. After half an hour, knead the dough lightly again and divide it into 10 equal portions. Roll each portion into a ball and set aside.
4. Sprinkle some flour onto the rolling surface you will be using.
5. Turn two rings on while you roll the *chapatis*. On one ring, put the *tava*/griddle. Keep the second to puff the *chapati*.
6. Take one ball at a time and roll in the flour you have set aside. Shake off any excess flour. Flatten the ball on the surface and roll it out into a circle of about 6" diameter (you may need to dip the disc into the flour once/twice while you roll).
7. Place the *roti* on the *tava*. Once the surface begins to show small bubbles, flip over and cook till brown spots appear.
8. Using tongs (*chimta*), lift the *phulka* and hold it over the second burner, allowing it to puff up. Once puffed, turn over immediately and allow the other side to cook for a few seconds.
9. Remove from the heat and place on a serving plate and apply a little *ghee* to one side before serving.

NOTES
- ✓ The kneading of the dough should be a gentle and slow process with water being incorporated into it little by little. If the dough is made too quickly, it may stick into a ball (giving the impression of being cohesive), but the *phulka*s made with it will not remain soft and will dry out fast.
- ✓ To make the *roti*s softer, some people add ½ tsp of oil while kneading the dough. Alternatively, a mix of milk and water (50:50) can be used when kneading the dough.
- ✓ In case you are cooking on an electric burner, place a cake cooling rack over the hob and use it to rest the *phulka*s on while they puff up.

SADA PARATHA
Plain Shallow-Fried Flat Bread

The Chhandyoga Upanishad (6.6.1-3,4) says: *Of the curd* (yogurt) *that is being churned that which is the subtlest part rises upwards and that becomes butter. So also, of the food that is eaten that which is the subtlest part rises upwards and that becomes the mind. Of the water that is drunk that which is the subtlest part rises upwards and that becomes* Prana....Hence, mind is made up of food, Prana *is made up of water.*

INGREDIENTS

2 ¼ cups whole-wheat flour (*atta*)
½ tsp salt (*namak*)
1 tbsp oil, for the dough (*tel*)
3-4 tbsp oil, for shallow frying (*tel*)
1 cup water

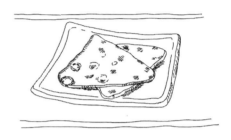

88

METHOD

1. Set aside ¼ cup flour for use when rolling the *parathas*.
2. Mix the flour, salt and oil and knead into a dough, adding a little water at a time. The dough is ready when it pulls away smoothly from the *paraat*/ bowl. Cover with a moist cloth and leave to rest for half an hour.
3. After half an hour, knead the dough lightly again and divide it into 10 equal portions. Roll each portion into a ball and set aside.
4. Sprinkle some flour on the rolling surface you will be using.
5. Take one ball at a time and roll in the flour you have set aside. Shake off any excess flour. Flatten the ball on the surface and roll into a circle of about 2" in diameter.
6. Apply a light layer of oil to half the circle of dough and fold over.
7. Again, apply oil to half the semi circle and fold into a quarter and press the layers together lightly with your fingers.
8. Dip the quarter into the flour set aside for rolling and shake off the excess. Roll into a triangle (you may need to sprinkle some flour while you roll).
9. Heat a *tava*/griddle on medium heat and place a rolled out *paratha*. Once the surface shows small bubbles, flip over. Apply oil with a very light hand to coat.

10. Turn over and apply oil to the other side.
11. Cook on medium heat till the *paratha* puffs up at the centre and turns golden brown with light brown spots on both sides.
12. Serve hot with fresh yoghurt.

BHARA PARATHA
Stuffed Shallow-Fried Flat Bread

INGREDIENTS
2 ¼ cups whole-wheat flour (*atta*)
½ tsp salt (*namak*)
1 tbsp oil, for the dough (*tel*)
3-4 tbsp oil, for shallow frying (*tel*)
1 cup water
4-5 medium-sized potatoes, boiled, peeled & grated (*alu*)
1-2 green chillies, chopped fine (*hari mirch*)
2 tbsp peeled & grated fresh ginger (*adrak*)
¼ tsp *garam masala*
¼ tsp pomegranate powder (*anardana* powder)
2 tbsp chopped, fresh coriander (*dhania patta*)

METHOD

1. Add the green chillies, ginger, coriander, *garam masala*, pomegranate powder and ¼ tsp salt to the potatoes and mix well.
2. Set aside ¼ cup flour for use when rolling the *parathas*.
3. Mix the flour, salt and oil and knead into a dough, adding a little water at a time. The dough is ready when it pulls away smoothly from the *paraat*/bowl. Cover with a moist cloth and leave to rest for half an hour.
4. After half an hour, knead the dough lightly again and divide it into 10 equal portions. Roll each portion into a ball and set aside.
5. Sprinkle some flour on the rolling surface you will be using.
6. Take one ball at a time and roll in the flour you have set aside. Shake off any excess flour. Flatten the ball on the surface and roll into a circle of about 3" in diameter.
7. Take about a tablespoon of the filling and place in the centre of the disc and fold the edges on all sides to seal. Dip lightly into the dry flour before rolling out to a disc of 5-6" diameter.
8. Heat a *tava*/griddle on medium heat and place the rolled-out *paratha*.
9. Cook on each side for about 2 minutes, applying a light coating of oil on both sides. Remove once the *paratha* is golden brown on both sides with brown spots.
10. Serve hot with fresh yoghurt.

NOTE

✓ Stuffed *parathas* can be made using a variety of fillings including finely grated cauliflower or radish.

BAJRA ROTI
Pearl Millet Flour Bread

The body requires no medicine if you eat only after the food you have already eaten is digested. ~Thirukural

INGREDIENTS
1/3 cup whole-wheat flour (*atta*)
1 cup pearl millet flour (*bajri ki atta*)
¼ tsp salt (*namak*)
1 tbsp oil (*tel*)

METHOD
1. Mix the *bajra* flour, wheat flour, oil and salt together. Add water, a little at a time, to make a soft dough. Lightly oil your hands and coat the dough. Cover with a moist cloth and leave to rest for about half an hour.
2. Divide into equal portions and roll into balls.
3. Roll out each ball into a disc of about 6" diameter.
4. Heat a *tava*/griddle on medium heat and place the rolled-out *roti* on it.
5. Cook on both sides till brown spots appear.
6. Lightly coat with *ghee* and serve hot.

NOTES
✓ The bread is both filling and a good source of energy. It is particularly suitable for *Pitta* and *Kapha* constitutions.
✓ It combines well with *baingan bharta*.

RAGI ROTI
Finger Millet Flour Bread

INGREDIENTS

1½ cups finger millet flour (*ragi ki atta*)
2-3 tbsp grated coconut (*nariyal*)
½ tsp mustard seeds (*rai*)
1 green chilli, chopped fine (*hari mirch*)
2-3 tbsp chopped, fresh coriander (*dhania patta*)
Salt to taste (*namak*)
4 tbsp oil (*tel*)
Warm water, to make a medium-soft dough

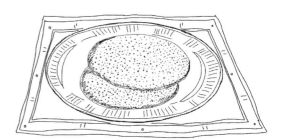

METHOD

92

1. Roast the *ragi* flour in a frying pan/*kadhai* on medium heat for 3-4 minutes. Remove the flour and set aside.
2. Wipe the same pan clean and heat ½ teaspoon oil and the mustard seeds. Once they splutter, add the green chillies and give it a quick stir. Take off the heat and add the chopped coriander and salt. Mix well.
3. Add 1 teaspoon more oil, then add this tempering to the roasted flour. Mix well.
4. Add the warm water to the flour, little by little, and knead into a soft dough. Cover with a moist cloth and set aside for half an hour.
5. Divide the dough into 7-8 equal-sized portions and roll into balls.
6. Oil the surface on which the *rotis* will be made.
7. Take one ball at a time and roll out into a disc of 6" diameter (approx). These *rotis* should be thicker than regular *phulkas*.
8. Heat a *tava*/griddle on medium heat and place the rolled out *ragi roti* on it. Cook on both sides, brushing lightly with oil. Serve hot.

NOTES
- ✓ *Ragi* balances all three *dosha*s and is very nourishing.
- ✓ Chopped onions are popularly added to the dough for this *roti*. Grated carrots/ bottle gourd are also an option.
- ✓ In case ragi flour does not appeal to your palate, mix in some wheat flour.
- ✓ Some people prefer to roll the rotis out on a sheet of plastic.

AKI KI ROTI
Rice Flour Bread

INGREDIENTS
1¼ cups rice flour *(akiki)*
1½ cups hot water OR milk *(dudh)*
2 tsp oil *(tel)*
A pinch of salt *(namak)*

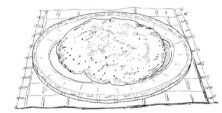

METHOD
1. Mix the oil into the rice flour, rubbing lightly with your fingers. Knead the rice flour with the hot water or milk till a soft dough forms. Set aside to rest for half an hour, covered with a moist cloth.
2. Divide the dough into equal-sized portions and roll into balls. Take one ball and roll it out into a disc of about 6" diameter, dusting with dry rice flour. These *roti*s should be thicker than regular *phulkas*.
3. Heat a *tava*/griddle on medium heat and place the rolled rice flour *roti* on it.
4. Dry roast the *roti* on both sides and serve hot.

NOTES
- ✓ If the *roti* seems to dry up on the *tava* even before it has cooked, use a moist cloth to dampen the upper surface of the *roti* while the underside cooks, then flip over.
- ✓ Grated capsicum, carrot and coconut can be added to the *roti* dough, along with cumin seeds and chopped green chillies.

JAWAR BHAKHRI
Sorghum Flour Bread

INGREDIENTS

1¼ cups sorgum flour (*jawar ki atta*)
¾ cup hot water
A pinch of salt (*namak*)

METHOD

1. Set aside ¼ cup flour to use while rolling the *bhakhri*. To the rest of the flour, add the hot water, a little at a time, kneading to form a soft dough. Cover with a moist cloth and leave to rest for half an hour.
2. Divide the dough into equal-sized portions and roll into balls.
3. Take one ball at a time and roll into a disc of about 6" diameter, dusting with some dry flour. These *rotis* should be thicker than regular *phulkas*.
4. Heat a *tava*/griddle on medium heat and place the rolled *bhakhri* on it.
5. Dry roast the *roti* on both sides and serve hot.

NOTES

✓ In case the *roti* seems to dry up on the *tava* even before it has cooked, use a moist cloth to dampen the upper surface of the *roti* while the underside cooks and then flip it over.
✓ These *rotis* are more brittle and fragile than the normal *chapatis*, hence they need to be handled with greater care when being rolled and transferred to the *tava*.

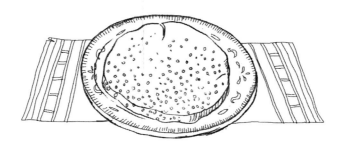

94

POORI
Wheat Flour Puffed Fried Bread

INGREDIENTS

1 cup whole-wheat flour (*atta*)
A pinch of salt (*namak*)
2 cups oil, for the dough, to roll & for frying (*tel*)
2/3 cup warm water

METHOD

1. Mix the flour, salt and 2 teaspoonfuls of oil, rubbing gently with your fingers. Add the warm water and knead to form a smooth dough. Cover with a moist cloth and set aside for 20-30 minutes.
2. Divide the dough into 7-8 equal portions and roll each into a ball.
3. Lightly apply oil to the rolling surface and the rolling pin. Meanwhile, put the remaining oil into a *kadhai*/frying pan and heat.
4. Take one ball at a time, flatten it with the palm of your hand and roll into a disc of about 4" diameter.
5. To check whether the oil is ready, drop a tiny bit of dough into it. If it rises to the surface almost immediately, the oil is hot enough.
6. Slide the *poori* into the *kadhai* from the side. Once it starts cooking, gently press on it with a slotted spoon (it should puff up).
7. Once light brown, turn over onto the other side and cook till done.
8. Remove from the oil, drain well and serve hot.

NOTES

✓ The dough can be flavoured with carom seeds to make *namak ajwain ki poori*.
✓ Potato curry, and sweet & sour yellow pumpkin, are traditional accompaniments to *poori* in north India.

DESSERTS

Cow's milk is considered to contain the core goodness of all plant life on the planet. Freshly churned butter and the ghee made from this milk, represents the essence of milk. According to tradition, just as the Divine is present within all creation, though hidden from view, to be realized only by the Sattvik mind, ghee is present within milk but invisible till Agni is introduced through churning and heating.

Ayurvedic practitioners explain that the quality of milk, as well as the process adopted to obtain butter, is crucial to making the best ghee. Organic whole milk from healthy, happy cows, duly churned (not extruded), and heated, will produce the best ghee. Fresh butter and ghee are both considered natural restoratives.

The famous Tirupati laddoos are made of besan, sugar, sugar-candy, cashewnuts, cardamom, raisins and ghee. The tradition of offering laddoos to Lord Venkateswara, started about 300 years ago. Nearly 200,000 laddoos are prepared daily at the temple by hereditary priests called archakas.

- Sooji Halwa
- Shrikhand
- Semiyan Payasam
- Rabdi
- Til Patti
- Pua
- Sweet Pongal

SOOJI HALWA
Hot Semolina Dessert

INGREDIENTS
1 cup vermicelli (*sooji*)
½ cup clarified butter (*ghee*)
2½ cups warm water
1 ¼ cups sugar (*sakkar*)
½ tsp crushed green cardamom seeds (*hari elaichi*)
1 tbsp finely chopped almonds (*badam*)

METHOD
1. Heat the *ghee* in a *kadhai* and add the *sooji*. Stir continuously on medium heat till the *sooji* emits a fragrant aroma and turns pinkish-brown.
2. Add the warm water and mix well. Once the mixture comes to the boil, reduce the heat so that it simmers. Add the sugar and half the cardamom powder.
3. Reduce the heat to low and cook for 2-3 minutes and keep stirring.
4. Turn the heat off and cover. Let it rest or 5 minutes.
5. Sprinkle the remaining cardamom powder and finely chopped almonds and serve hot.

SHRIKHAND
Fruit & Saffron Yoghurt

INGREDIENTS
4 cups fresh yoghurt (*dahi*)
2 cups mango purée (*aam*)
4 tbsp sugar (*sakkar*)
5 strands saffron, soaked in 1 tbsp milk (*zaffran dudh*)
½ tsp crushed green cardamom seeds (*hari elaichi*)
1 tsp finely chopped almonds (*badam*)

METHOD
1. Hang the yoghurt, tied in a fine muslin cloth, for 2-3 hours, till all the excess water has drained away.
2. Mix together the yoghurt, saffron, sugar and mango purée till the sugar has dissolved.
3. Sprinkle the cardamom powder and chopped almonds and serve chilled.

SEMIYAN PAYASAM
Vermicelli Pudding

Teertham, *the consecrated water offered to devotees in temples in south India, is made by mixing in 1 litre of pure water, 1 tsp cardamom powder, ½ tsp clove powder, a pinch of* pachai karpooram, *7-8* tulsi *leaves, and a couple of strands of saffron. The resulting liquid should be stored in copper containers. Taken twice a day, up to 2 tsp at a time, it acts as a mouth freshener, keeps teeth and gums healthy, and is said to facilitate sound sleep.*

INGREDIENTS

2 litres milk, preferably full cream (*dudh*)

¾ cup vermicelli (*semiyan*)

½ cup sugar (*sakkar*)

5 strands saffron (*zaffran*)

2 tbsps broken cashewnuts (*kaju*)

15-16 raisins (*kishmish*)

¼ tsp cardamom powder (*elaich*)

1-2 tbsp clarified butter (*ghee*)

99

METHOD

Bring the milk to a boil in a deep saucepan and thicken on low heat for about 10 minutes. Keep stirring from time to time.

Soak the saffron in 1 tablespoon of hot milk and set aside.

In half the *ghee*, brown the cashew pieces. Remove and set aside.

Add the raisins and stir for a few seconds till they puff up. Remove and set aside.

In a frying pan, heat the remaining *ghee* and fry the vermicelli on medium heat for a minute. Add 1 cup water and cook till the vermicelli is tender but not too soft.

Add the sugar and mix until dissolved.

Pour in the milk, followed by the cardamom powder and saffron. Mix well.

Simmer on low heat for 4-5 minutes. Remove from heat and garnish with the cashews and raisins before serving.

NOTES
- ✓ Saffron has been classified as amongst the most *sattvik* of spices and a little goes a long way. To release the full aroma and colour, it is recommended that the milk-soaked strands of saffron should be pressed to release its juices.
- ✓ In southern India, a pinch of camphor added to the *payasam* in place of saffron, gives a unique flavour

100

Teertham (Consecrated Water)

RABDI
Slow-Cooked Thick Milk Pudding

The Tamil word for sesame, gingelly, *is thought to have originated around the 8ʰ century AD and comes from the Arabic word,* juljul *or* jeljel, *to signify the rattling sound made by the seeds in the sesame pods.*

INGREDIENTS

1 litre full cream milk (*dudh*)
3-4 tbsp sugar (*sakkar*)
1 tbsp rosewater (*gulabjal*)

METHOD

1. Take a wide-mouthed, heavy-bottomed frying pan/*kadhai* and heat the milk till it comes to a boil. Once the milk is boiling, lower the heat and allow it to simmer and thicken on gentle heat. While the milk is simmering, a layer of creamy skin will keep forming on the surface. Remove this layer every few minutes and push it to the side of the vessel. Reduce the milk till it is about a quarter of the original volume.
2. Mix in the sugar till it dissolves and scrape the sides of the vessel to mix all the solidified cream.
3. Remove from heat and allow to cool to room temperature before adding the rosewater and mixing it in.
4. Serve slightly chilled.

NOTE

✓ A pinch of crushed cardamom seeds could be added as a garnish

TIL PATTI

Sesame-Jaggery Thins

Sugar has an increasingly cooler effect as it gets refined. It also becomes more difficult to digest, hence the use of jaggery during winter to add sweetness to beverages like ginger tea.

INGREDIENTS

2 cups crumbled jaggery (*gur*)
2 cups sesame seeds (*til*)
2 tsps clarified butter (*ghee*)

METHOD

1. In a heavy-bottomed pan, roast the sesame seeds on gentle heat till they give off an aroma and turn light brown. Do not over-cook them or they will turn bitter. Remove from heat and set aside. Once cooled, crush them roughly.
2. Clean and lightly grease a wooden board or the kitchen counter, to use as a setting surface for the *til patti*.
3. Heat 1 teaspoon of *ghee* in the same heavy-bottomed pan and add the jaggery pieces. Once it melts, cook on gentle heat for 2 minutes before adding the crushed sesame seeds. Mix well.
4. Turn the mixture out onto the greased surface and wait till it has cooled enough to be rolled out.
5. Use a greased rolling pin to flatten the mixture and roll out as thin as you want. Mark a grid on the surface of the *til-patti* and leave to cool and set.
6. Pry the hardened *til-patti* away from the surface once it is cool and break into individual pieces. Store in an airtight container and serve as required.

NOTE

✓ Jaggery and sesame are both warming, hence this sweet is popular during cooler weather.

PUA
Wheat Flour Fritters

The word pua, *traces its origin to the sweet barley cakes called* apupa, *which have been eaten from Vedic times. These cakes were often dipped in honey.*

INGREDIENTS

2 cups whole wheat flour (*atta*)

½ cup sugar (*sakkar*)

1½ cups milk (*dudh*)/ water

Oil/clarified butter (*ghee*), for frying

METHOD

1. Mix in the sugar and water (or milk), till dissolved.
2. Make a smooth batter by combining the flour with the sweetened milk/water.
3. The batter should be the dropping consistency used for *pakoras*.
4. Beat gently, cover and set the batter aside for 10-15 minutes.
5. Meanwhile, heat the *ghee*/oil in a *kadhai* for frying.
6. To check whether the oil is ready, drop a little batter into it. If the piece rises to the surface almost immediately, the oil is hot enough.
7. Scoop up the batter by cupping the fingers of your hand and drop into the hot oil/*ghee*. Drop between 4-6 *pua*s into the *kadhai* at a time and fry till red-brown.
8. Remove with a slotted spoon and drain to remove excess oil.
9. Serve hot.

104

Sweet Pongal
Rice & Yellow Mung Beans Dessert
This dish is traditionally cooked during the festival of Pongal *and is offered first to the Gods.*

INGREDIENTS
1 cup rice (*chawal*)
½ cup mung lentil, split & dehusked (*moong dal*)
1½ cups crushed & powdered jaggery (*gur*)
¼ -½ tsp powdered green cardamom seeds (*hari elaichi*)
3 tbsp broken cashewnuts (*kaju*)
3 tbsp raisins (*kishmish*)
¼ cup clarified butter (*ghee*)
3 cups milk (*dudh*)
2 cups water

105

METHOD
1. In a frying pan, heat 1 teaspoon *ghee* and gently roast the yellow *moong dal* till it emits an aroma and turns pink. Remove from heat and set aside.
2. In the same pan, heat 2 teaspoons *ghee* and add the cashews and raisins. Fry gently, stirring constantly till the cashews turn golden and the raisins swell. Remove and set aside.
3. Put the rice and *dal* into a pressure cooker. Add the milk and water and cook till tender (if you have time, this can be done in a pan, simmering slowly).
4. In a pan, add the jaggery and 1 cup water. Cook on medium heat till the jaggery has melted. Once the mixture has come to a rolling boil, turn down the heat and simmer for about 5 minutes. Set aside.
5. Add the cooked *dal* and rice mixture to the jaggery syrup, followed by the raisins, cashewnuts, cardamom powder and *ghee*. Mix well on gentle heat till the mixture blends together and looks and feels sticky. Cover and let it rest for 10 mins before serving. Finely chopped coconut pieces (fried in *ghee*), can also be added.

NAIVEDYAM & FESTIVAL FOODS

Sri Ram ~ Gift of Agni: *Dasharath, King of Ayodhya, had three wives – Kaushalya, Sumitra and Kaikeyi. None of them bore any children. So the King performed a homa or havan, to pray for progeny. As a reward, Agni, the Fire God, gave him three portions of payas – a sweet which his queens would eat and so conceive divine children. When each of the queens received her share, Kaikeyi dropped hers by mistake and the payas was blown away by Vayu, the Wind God. He dropped it into the willing hands of Anjani, a she-monkey, who ate it and gave birth to the powerful Hanuman or Anjaneya, who leapt to catch the shining sun in the sky. The sun, chased into the firmament by this divine power, gave Hanuman golden garments which could be seen only by Rama and thus enable him to recognise his greatest devotee. Kaushalya and Sumitra gave half of their payas to the grieving Kaikeyi. In fulfilment of the boon granted by Agni, the queens gave birth to Rama, Lakshmana, Bharat and Shatrughna. The latter two were twins, born to Kaikeyi, who had received two halves of the* payas.

- Sabudana Khichdi
- Samva ke Chawal
- Kootu ki Pakodi
- Ras ke Alu
- Lauki ka Raita
- Kootu ki Poori
- Kasaar
- Sabudana Vada
- Singhaade ke Aate ki Barfi

SABUDANA KHICHDI
Sago Pearl Stir-Fry

Panchamrit, from panch *or 'five' +* amrita *or 'nectar', forms an essential part of* pujas *as an offering to the Gods. Mix together: 1 litre cow's milk, 100gm curd, 2 tsp honey, 1 tsp melted clarified butter* (ghee) *and 100gm sugar. Mix together and refrigerate. Now the* Panchamrit *is ready to be used for* bhog.

INGREDIENTS

1 cup sago pearls (*sabudana*)
2 medium-sized potatoes, boiled & cubed (*alu*)
¼ cup peanuts, skinned, roasted & lightly crushed (*mungfalli*)
1 tsp cumin seeds (*jeera*)
2 green chillies, finely chopped (*hari mirch*)
3-4 curry leaves (*kari patta*)
1 tbsp clarified butter (*ghee*)
1 tsp lemon juice, optional (*limbu*)
2 tbsp finely chopped, fresh coriander (*dhania patta*)
2 tbsp freshly grated coconut (*nariyal*)
1 pinch sugar (*sakkar*)
Salt to taste (*namak*)

METHOD

1. Soak the *sabudana* overnight in just enough water to cover it. In the morning, it should be soft and fluffy with no extra water remaining. Set aside. OR soak the *sabudana* for half an hour in enough water. Drain and leave to rest overnight.

2. Heat oil in a frying pan/*kadhai*. Add the cumin seeds. Once they splutter, add the chopped green chillies and curry leaves. After a quick stir add the potatoes, salt, sugar and peanuts followed by the *sabudana*. Cook together for 5 mins on low to medium heat. The *sabudana* should be translucent when done.

3. Add the crushed peanuts, grated coconut and chopped coriander as garnish. Serve hot.

NOTES

✓ Once the *sabudana* is soaked, the salt, sugar and lime juice can be mixed with it directly if desired.

✓ Instead of using boiled potatoes, thinly sliced and diced raw potatoes can also be used. The cooking time for the same will need to be increased appropriately.

✓ Chopped cucumber can be added to the *khichdi*.

✓ *Sabudana* comes in different sizes, the larger pearls are better for making *khichdi*.

108

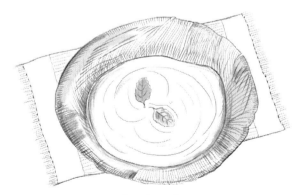

Panchamrit

SAMVA KE CHAWAL
Indian Wild Rice

Atithi Devo Bhava: *Feeding the* atithi *(guest), is indicative of the offering made to the* Vaishvanara. 'Aham vaishvaanaro bhutva praninaam deham ashritah ; Praan apaan samayuktah pachami annam chaturvidham' *(Based in the body of living beings, I manifest as the digestive Fire, Vaishvaanara; in combination with the vital energies known as Prana and Apana, I digest the four kinds of food consumed by them), Lord Krishna declares in the* Bhagavad Gita 15:14.

INGREDIENTS
½ cup Indian wild rice (*samva ke chawal*)
1½ cups water
1 medium-sized potato, boiled (*alu*)
1 tbsp clarified butter (*ghee*)
6-8 black peppercorns, crushed roughly (*kala mirch*)
Rock salt to taste (*sendha namak*)
2 tsp finely chopped fresh coriander (*dhania patta*)

METHOD
1. Crush the boiled potato with your hands and set aside.
2. In a frying pan/*kadhai*, heat the *ghee* and add the peppercorns and potatoe. Give it a quick stir. Add the water and rock salt and bring to a boil.
3. Put in the *samva ke chawal* and mix well. Allow the mixture to come to a boil before turning the heat down. Cook on low to medium heat till the water ishas been absorbed and the rice is done. Garnish with chopped coriander. Serve hot.

NOTES
✓ This dish is generally cooked in north India during the *Navratri* period.
✓ The spices and garnishes used can be adjusted depending on individual preferences / family traditions (eg. some families add green chillies, cumin seeds, ginger, cardamom and cloves).

KOOTU KI PAKODI
Buckwheat Flour Fritters

Phalahar: *for ritual purposes, all crops raised with the help of the plough, were termed* anna *or* kristapachya. *Food that grew without cultivation was called* phala *or* akristapachya. *The latter included wild grains, vegetables and fruits. Only the latter category was permitted during rituals and fasts, hence the food that falls into the category of* phalahar.

INGREDIENTS

1 cup buckwheat flour (*kootu atta*)
1 cup potato, boiled, peeled & roughly broken up (*alu*)
¼ tsp crushed black peppercorns (*kala mirch*)
Rock salt to taste (*sendha namak*)
Oil/ clarified butter for deep frying (*ghee*)

110

METHOD

1. Mix the black pepper and salt into the *kootu* flour.
2. Mix the crushed potatoes with the flour. Add water, a little at a time, so that the potatoes are coated with a thick batter.
3. Heat the *ghee*/oil in a *kadhai*/frying pan. Once the oil is hot, drop a small piece of the batter into it – if it rises almost immediately, the oil is ready. Drop 4-5 *pakoris* at a time into the oil and fry till golden brown and crisp. Remove with a slotted spoon and drain.
4. Serve hot with green chutney

NOTES

✓ Adjust the spices for the *samva ke chawal* according to personal preference.
✓ The *pakodis* provide a crisp accompaniment to *samva ke chawal* and fresh yoghurt.

RAS KE ALU
Simple Potato Curry

Kachcha khana & pukka khana: *the foods cooked in water are categorized as* kachcha khana *eg.* dal, *rice and* khichdi. Pukka khana *comprises foodstuffs cooked with fat (generally ghee). In the latter class, the first contact of the foodstuff* (anna *or* phala), *is with the* ghee *or oil. Thus, rice* kheer, *in which the rice is first fried in* ghee *before being cooked in milk and sugar, come under* pukka *food. If rice is added to milk first, despite the addition of sugar and* ghee *later, this will class it as* doodh-bhaat, *which is* kachcha khana.

INGREDIENTS

2-3 medium-sized potatoes, boiled & peeled (*alu*)

1 tbsp clarified butter (*ghee*)

6-8 black peppercorns, crushed (*kala mirch*)

2 tsp tamarind paste (*imli*)

Rock salt to taste (*sendha namak*)

111

METHOD

1. Break the potatoes roughly, using your hands. Set aside.
2. Heat the *ghee* in a *kadhai* and add the crushed black pepper. Give it a quick stir.
3. Add the potatoes and mix well.
4. Add the salt and 1 cup of water.
5. Allow the curry to come to a boil and then simmer for a couple of minutes before adding the tamarind paste. Mix well and take off the heat.
6. Serve hot with *kootu poori*s or *samva ke chawal* (refer Contents).

NOTE

✓ For the *samva ke chawal*, adjust the spices according to personal preference.

LAUKI KA RAITA
Spicy Yoghurt with Grated Bottle Gourd

INGREDIENTS
1 cup peeled & grated bottle gourd (*lauki*)
2 cups yoghurt (*dahi*)
¼ tsp crushed black peppercorns (*kala mirch*)
Rock salt to taste (*sendha namak*)

METHOD
1. Boil 1 cup water and blanch the bottle gourd till tender. Drain and set aside.
2. Whisk the yoghurt with the black pepper and rock salt.
3. Mix in the blanched bottle gourd.
4. Serve at room temperature or slightly chilled.

112

NOTES
✓ A variation of this *raita* can be made using with yellow pumpkin (*kaddu*).
✓ Adjust the spices according to personal taste (eg. add roasted and ground cumin seeds to enhance the flavour of the *raita*).

KOOTU KI POORI
Buckwheat Flour Puffed Fried Bread

Bhog *&***Prasad**: *anything offered to God during worship can be* bhog. *The word denotes enjoyment or pleasure, and the devotee offers what he can to please the deity. Once the offering has been made, it becomes blessed and is referred to as* prasad. *Consuming this* prasad *in silence allows all the beneficial qualities of the food to permeate our being.*

INGREDIENTS

1 ¼ cups buckwheat flour (*kootu atta*)
1 cup boiled, peeled & grated potato (*alu*)
A pinch of rock salt (*sendha namak*)
¼ tsp crshed black peppercorns (*kala mirch*)
Oil/ clarified butter for deep frying (*ghee*)

METHOD

1. Set aside ¼ cup kootu atta for rolling. Mix the black pepper and rock salt into the remaining *atta*.
2. Add the grated boiled potatoes and knead into a smooth dough (no water needs to be added to this dough as the moisture in the potatoes or colocasia will suffice).
3. Cover the dough with a moist cloth and allow to rest for 15-20 minutes.
4. Divide the dough into 5-6 equal portions, roll into balls and set aside.
5. Take one ball at a time, dip into some dry flour and flatten, using the palms of your hands. Roll into a disc of about 5-6" diameter. Set aside and do the same for the others portions.
6. Heat *ghee*/oil in a frying pan/*kadhai*. To check if the oil is hot enough, drop a small piece of the dough into the oil – if it rises to the surface almost immediately, the oil is ready.
7. Slide a *poori* into the hot oil and fry till golden brown. Remove with a slotted spoon, drain and set aside. Fry all in the same way and serve hot.

KASAAR
Wheat Flour Roasted in Clarified Butter with Chopped Fruit

Chhappan Bhog: it is said that Lord Krishna partook of 8 meals a day. When he lifted the Mount Govardhan for seven days to protect the people from the wrath of Indra, he was unable to eat. When the episode ended with Indra surrendering, the grateful populace offered bhog to the Lord for the days he had been without food and thus came about the term chhapan bhog.

INGREDIENTS

2½ cups whole-wheat flour (*atta*)
2-3 tbsp semolina (*sooji*)
1-2 tbsp clarified butter (*ghee*)
1¼ cups fine grained sugar (*sakkar*)
6-7 almonds, chopped fine (*badam*)
20-25 raisins (*kishmish*)
½ tsp cardamom powder (*elaichi*)
1½ cups chopped mixed fruit - bananas, apples, guavas (*phal*)
½ tsp lemon juice (*limbu*)

114

METHOD

1. Add the lemon juice to the chopped fruit and mix well. Set aside.
2. In a *kadhai*, heat the *ghee* and add the *atta* and *sooji* and roast on medium heat until it emits an aroma and turns pinkish. Remove from heat and set aside to cool.
3. Once the mixture is cool, add the sugar, raisins, almonds and cardamom powder and mix well.
4. Add in the chopped fruits just before serving.

NOTES

✓ This is a traditional *prasad* offered after prayers or *katha* in north India.
✓ Peeled melon seeds and roasted *makhana* (fox nuts), can also be added.

CHHAPPAN BHOG

Chhappan Bhog at the Jagannatha Puri Temple comprises the following dishes.

1. Ukhuda (Sweet puffed rice)
2. Nadia kora (Coconut laddu)
3. Khua (Slow cooked dried milk)
4. Dahi (Yoghurt)
5. Pachila kadali (Ripe Banana)
6. Kanika (Flavoured Rice)
7. Tata Khechudi (Dry Khechudi)
8. Mendha Mundia (Cake)
9. Bada Kanti (Fried Cake)
10. Matha Puli (Pancake)
11. Hamsa Keli (Sweet cake)
12. Jhili (Thin pan cake like Dosa)
13. Enduri (Idli)
14. Adapachedi (Ginger Paste)
15. Saga Bhaja (Fried greens)
16. Kadali Bhaja (Fried Plantain)
17. Maric Ladu (Pepper laddus)
18. San Pitha (Small size cake)
19. Bara (Deep-fried dumplings)
20. Arisha (Fried rice-flour cake)
21. Bundia (Gram flour drops in syrup)
22. Pakhal (Rice cooked with water)
23. Khiri (Rice cooked with milk)
24. Kadamba (Sweet)
25. Pat Manohar (Sweet)
26. Takuaa (Tongue-shaped sweets)
27. Bhaga Pitha (Sweet fried cake)
28. Gotai (Salty cake)
29. Dalma (Dal with vegetables)
30. Kakara (Wheat-flour pasties)
31. Luni Khuruma (Salty Biscuits)
32. Amalu (Malpua, Sweet Puri)
33. Suar Pitha (Baked Cake)
34. Biri Buha (Black gram cake)
35. Jhadai Nadaa (Tiny cakes)
36. Khasta Puri (Crisp fried cakes)
37. Kadali Bara (Fried Plantains)
38. Sana Arisha (Small fried cakes)
39. Sakar (Chutney)
40. Podo Pitha (Panned Cake)
41. Kanji (Sour Rice)
42. Dahi Pakhal (Curd rice)
43. Bada Arisha (Large fried cake)
44. Tipuri (Three stage fillings)
45. Sakara (Sugar candy)
46. Suji Khir (Milk with semolina)
47. Muga Sijha (Boiled green gram)
48. Manohar (Sweet)
49. Magaja Ladu (Laddus with dried musk-melon seeds)
50. Pana (Sweet Drink)
51. Anna (Rice)
52. Ghia Anna (Rice with bengal gram)
53. Dali (Sweet Dal)
54. Besar (Mixed veg. curry)
55. Mahur (Vegetable curry with mustard seeds)
56. Sag (Leafy vegetables)

Balaram, Jagannath and Subhadra, the deities enshrined at Jagannath Temple, Puri

SABUDANA VADA
Sago Pearl Fritters

INGREDIENTS

1 cup sago (*sabudana*)
1 cup boiled, peeled & grated potato (*alu*)
¼ cup peanuts, roasted & crushed (*mungfalli*)
1 tsp cumin seeds (*jeera*)
1 green chilli, chopped fine (*hari mirch*)
Salt to taste (*namak*)
Oil for deep frying (*tel*)

METHOD

1. Soak the *sabudana* in just enough water to cover it. Leave overnight. In the morning, it should be soft and fluffy with no extra water remaining. Set aside.
2. Mix the *sabudana* with the grated potato, chopped green chilli, crushed peanuts, cumin seeds and salt, and form a dough.
3. Divide into equal-sized portions and make into patties.
4. Heat oil in a *kadhai* and slide the *vada*s into the hot oil one by one. Deep fry till golden brown. Remove with a slotted spoon and drain on paper towels.
5. Serve hot with green chutney.

SINGHAADE KE AATE KI BARFI
Water Chestnut Flour Pudding

INGREDIENTS

1 cup water chestnut flour (*singhade ka atta*)
1 cup sugar (*sakkar*)
1-2 tbsp clarified butter (*ghee*)
¼ tsp finely crushed green cardamom seeds (*hari elaichi*)
3 cups water

METHOD

1. Use a teaspoon of the *ghee* to grease a *thali*. Set aside.
2. Heat the remaining *ghee* in a *kadhai* and add the *singhada atta*. Roast till it gives off an aroma and turns light pink.
3. Add the water and sugar and stir constantly till the sugar dissolves and the mixture comes to a boil. Cook for another 4-5 minutes on medium heat. The mixture will thicken as you do so.
4. Remove from heat and pour out onto the greased *thali*. Using a spatula, spread in a thick layer and allow to cool and set.
5. Cut into pieces using a knife and serve.

119

CHUTNEYS

UGADI PACHADI
Six-Tastes Chutney

The unique flavours of this pachadi *or chutney, is said to reflect the gamut of emotions we experience in life through the six rasas or emotions. The word* rasa, *is also commonly understood as taste and this chutney features the six tastes identified by Ayurveda – sweet, sour, salty, bitter, pungent and astringent. It is traditionally made at the start of the new year which is referred to as* Ugadi *in Karnataka, Maharashtra and Andhra Pradesh.*

INGREDIENTS

2 tsp *neem* flowers
4 tsp powdered/grated jaggery (*gur*)
1 tbsp finely chopped raw mango (*kaccha aam*)
¼ tsp red chilli powder (*lal mirch*)
2-3 tbsp thick tamarind pulp (*imli*)
½ tsp mustard seeds (*rai*)
1 tsp oil (*tel*)
Salt to taste (*namak*)

121

METHOD

✓ Dilute the tamarind pulp in ½ cup water, add the jaggery and mix.
✓ Add the chopped mango. Cook on medium heat till the mango becomes tender and the jaggery has dissolved.
✓ In a pan, heat the oil and add the mustard seeds. Once they splutter, add the *neem* flowers and fry till they turn a light brown.
✓ Add the salt and chilli powder and mix into the tamarind-mango mixture.
✓ Serve as an accompaniment.

NARIAL CHUTNEY
Coconut Chutney

INGREDIENTS

1 cup grated fresh coconut (*nariyal*)
½ cup gram *dal*, fried (*chana dal*)
1 green chilli (*hari mirch*)
1" piece fresh ginger, peeled (*adrak*)
2 tbsps tamarind paste (*imli*)
Salt to taste (*namak*)
1-2 tsp oil, for tempering (*vaghar tel*)
½ tsp mustard seeds (*rai*)
1 tsp de-husked, split black gram (*urad dal*)
1 dry red chilli, halved (*Kashmiri mirch*)
½ tsp asafoetida (*hing*)
4-6 fresh curry leaves (*kari patta*)

METHOD

1. Grind the coconut, fried gram *dal*, green chilli, fresh ginger and tamarind paste in a grinder, adding just enough water to make it a thick paste.
2. Add salt to taste and mix well.
3. In a frying pan, heat the oil and add the mustard seeds. Once they splutter, add the split black gram, dry red chilli, asafoetida and fresh curry leaves. Pour on to the coconut chutney and adjust seasoning if required.
4. Serve at room temperature.

Hari Chutney
Coriander Chutney

INGREDIENTS
2 cups fresh coriander leaves, thoroughly washed & drained (*dhania patta*)
1-2 green chillies (*hari mirch*)
1 tsp cumin seeds, roasted & powdered (*jeera*)
A pinch of asafoetida (*hing*)
½ tsp coriander powder (*dhania* powder)
Salt to taste (*namak*)
Lemon juice to taste (*limbu*)

METHOD

1. Grind the coriander leaves, green chillies, cumin seeds, asafoetida, coriander powder, salt and lemon juice, with a little water.
2. Serve at room temperature.

NOTES

1. During the summer months, ½ cup mint leaves can be added to the chutney before grinding to give a cool, fresh taste.
2. When available, raw mango or Indian gooseberry (*amla*), can be used in place of lemon juice as the souring agent.
3. To make **Tridoshic Green Chutney**: grind a bunch of fresh coriander with ¼ cup fresh lemon juice, ¼ cup water, ¼ cup grated coconut, 2 tbsp chopped fresh ginger, 1 tsp barley malt or raw honey and 1 tsp sea salt.

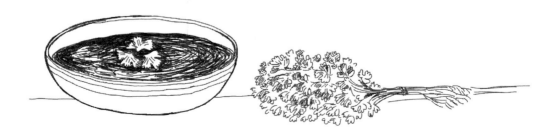

IMLI KI CHUTNEY
Tamarind Chutney

INGREDIENTS
2 cups tamarind pulp (*imli*)
3-3½ cups jaggery (*gur*)
1 tsp cumin seeds, roasted & powdered (*jeera*)
½ tsp red chilli powder (*lal mirch*)
Salt to taste (*namak*)
1 tsp powdered black salt (*kala namak*)
1 tsp *garam masala*

METHOD
1. Heat the tamarind pulp on medium heat. Add the grated jaggery, cumin powder, red chilli powder and then lower the heat. Keep stirring till the jaggery dissolves and the mixture starts to thicken.
2. Remove from the heat and add the salt and black salt.
3. Allow to cool and serve at room temperature.

125

THE NATURE OF COMMON FOODS

Dairy: organic dairy products have an inherently *sattvik* nature but pasteurization reduces the beneficial qualities of milk including its *sattvik* nature considerably.

Nuts and Seeds: are *sattvik* in nature but heavy to digest and therefore should be taken in small quantities. It is important to remember that rancid nuts or seeds are tamasik.

Fruits: can generally without exception be taken as *sattvik*. They are nourishing and cleansing and harmonizing.

Vegetables: most vegetables come only second to fruits when counting sattvik foods. Excess of any vegetables of the cabbage family (cauliflower, cabbage, broccoli etc), can be rajasik. Pungent vegetables (onions, garlic, chillies) are generally *rajasik* and *tamasik*.

Grains: are generally *sattvik* particularly long grained basmati rice or brown rice. Grain is preferred to bread because it provides slow and steady release of energy.

Beans: are nourishing but can be *rajasik* and are best consumed with spices.

Oils: *ghee* is the most *sattvik* cooking medium and enhances intelligence. Among the oils, sesame and coconut oils are regarded as *sattvik*.

Sweeteners: except the sweet in fruits and natural sweeteners such as honey sweeteners particularly refined sugars are *tamasic*.

GLOSSARY OF TERMS

Alu: Potato

Amchur: Dry, powdered unripe, green mangoes, used as a souring agent, particularly in north India.

Asafoetida/Asafetida: Dried resin from a rhizome. Available in powdered or solid form. Imparts a unique flavour apart from its many beneficial properties.

Ajwain: Bishop's Weed, Caraway or Carom Seeds. It has a flavour similar to Thyme due to the presence of thymol and is a valuable digestive aid.

Anardana: Pomegranate seeds, usually dried and powdered and used as a souring agent.

Adrak: Root ginger

Arhar/tur/tuvar: Pigeon peas

Atta: Whole wheat flour

Badam: Almonds

Besan: Chickpea flour, widely used in India as the flour of choice to make fritters because of its crispness when fried

Baingan: Eggplant, Brinjal

Bhutta: Corn

Choora/ Poha/ pauwa: Beaten, dehusked rice, generally soaked, roasted and beaten flat.

Chana: part of the lentil family, generally referred to as Bengal Gram. The smaller, dark-skinned and wrinkled variety is native to India whereas the paler, larger, and relatively smooth-skinned cousin (referred to as *Kabulichana*), is from the Mediterranean.

Chana dal: Split Bengal Gram. It is prepared by de-husking the whole *kala chana*.

Chat Masala: a popular spice mix made by combining powdered *amchur*, red chilli, coriander, cumin, asafoetida, dried ginger, black salt (*kala namak*) and regular salt. Can be added to /sprinkled over a wide range of dishes from *pakora*s to diced fruit.

Curry Leaves: small shiny, dark-green leaves with a unique aroma used as staple seasoning in south Indian and central Indian dishes. Also called *meetha neem/kadi patta*.

Chhuaara: Dried dates

Dahi: yoghurt
Dalchini: Cinnamon
Dalia: Crushed, pre-roasted and germinated wheat. Akin to bulgur wheat and used for both sweet and savoury preparations.
Dhania: Coriander

Elaichi (Badi): Black Cardamom
Elaichi (Chhoti): Green Cardamom

Garam Masala: a combination of ground or pounded dry spices, the constituents and proportion of which vary from kitchen to kitchen. Usually comprises cumin, coriander, cardamom, peppercorns, ginger powder, cloves, Bay leaves, nutmeg and mace.
Gahat/ Muthira/ Kulthi: Horse gram
Ghee: Clarified Butter

Hara Dhania/Dhania Patta: Fresh coriander
Hari Mirch: Green Chillies
Hing: Asafoetida

Imli: Tamarind

Jaiphal: Nutmeg
Javitri: Mace
Jeera: Cumin

Kadhai: a wok-shaped, thick, circular and deep cooking vessel with a heavy base. It is versatile and can be used for deep frying and cooking dishes with or without gravy.
Kaju: Cashewnut
Kokum: A slender, small and evergreen tree that belongs to the Mangosteen family. The fruit is popularly used as souring agent in peninsular India.
Kala Masala: also known as *Goda Masala* (a spice blend in Maharashtra and adjoining areas)

Kala Namak: Black (or Purple) Rock Salt. Has a pungent flavour and adds taste to yoghurt preparations. Use sparingly.

Kali Mirch: Black Peppercorn
Kari Patta: Curry Leaves
Kharbooze ke Beej/ Magaz: Musk Melon Seeds
Kheer: A dessert made by cooking rice/*rava*/vermicelli with milk and sugar.
Kheera: Cucumber
Kurmura/Murmura/ Muri/ Maramalu/Laiya: Puffed rice. Generally made by heating rice kernels under high pressure.
Lauki/Dudhi: Bottle Gourd or the Long Melon
Laung: Cloves

Malai: Milk cream
Maida: Refined white flour
Methi: Fenugreek, the leaves are used
Moong: Green Gram, part of the lentil family
Masoor: This *dal* is what is commonly referred to as lentils in the West. Usually has a brown skin and is pink-orange in colour when dehusked.
Mooli: Radish or a variety of east Asian Daikon
Moongphali: Groundnuts

Limbu/Nimbu ka Sat: Citric Acid

Paneer: Fresh Cottage Cheese
Paratha: Unleavened flat bread cooked on a *tava* with oil or *ghee*, and sometimes flavoured with carom seeds or stuffed with vegetables
Patta Gobhi: Cabbage
Phool Gobhi: Cauliflower
Phulka/Roti: Unleavened flat bread rolled out without use of oil and cooked on a *tava*.
Pippali: Long Pepper

Porridge: A dish made by cooking whole or broken cereals in milk, water or a mixture of both. Can be eaten as sweet or savoury
Pudina: Mint

Rice/ Boiled Rice: rice which has been partially boiled in the husk; used to make *idli-dosa* etc
Rai: Small Mustard Seeds
Rajma: Red Kidney Beans

Sabudana: Sago pearls
Sarson: Large Mustard Seeds
Saunf: Aniseed
Simla Mirch: Capsicum, Bell Peppers
Sooji/ Rava: Semolina, the granular form of endosperm of wheat produced during milling.
Salt/ Rock Salt: Salt found in sedimentary deposits and called *sendha namak* in north India. It is invariably used during religious fasts.
Salt/ Black Rock Salt: A variety of rock salt, also called *sanchal* or *kala namak*. It is pungent, has a purple colour and is often used in India to add a unique flavour to drinks. It is a part of *chat masala*.

Tava: A flat or slightly convex-shaped griddle used for cooking Indian flatbreads and pancakes. Traditionally made of cast iron, but is now widely available with non-stick coating. Dosa tava is generally flat whereas the one used for chapatis is often convex.
Tej Patta: Bay Leaf
Tuvar/ Arhar: Pigeon Peas. Part of the lentil family.

Urad: Black Gram. Part of the lentil family.

130